# The Hussites

# PAST IMPERFECT

Past Imperfect presents concise critical overviews of the latest research by the world's leading scholars. Subjects cross the full range of fields in the period ca. 400—1500 CE which, in a European context, is known as the Middle Ages. Anyone interested in this period will be enthralled and enlightened by these overviews, written in provocative but accessible language. These affordable paperbacks prove that the era still retains a powerful resonance and impact throughout the world today.

## Director and Editor-in-Chief

Simon Forde, *'s-Hertogenbosch*

## Production

Ruth Kennedy, *Adelaide*

# The Hussites

Stephen E. Lahey

ARC HUMANITIES PRESS

**British Library Cataloguing in Publication Data**
A catalogue record for this book is available from the British Library

© 2019, Arc Humanities Press, Leeds

ISBN (print): 9781641891622
e-ISBN (PDF): 9781641891639
e-ISBN (EPUB): 9781641891646

**www.arc-humanities.org**
Printed and bound by CPI Group (UK) Ltd, Croydon, CR0 4YY

# Contents

# Introduction

On his return from a meeting in Munich with Hitler in 1938, Neville Chamberlain famously said, "How horrible, fantastic, incredible it is, that we should be digging trenches and trying on gas masks here, because of a quarrel in a far away country between people of whom we know nothing." He was referring to tensions between ethnic Germans and Czechs in what was then Czechoslovakia which Hitler had used as an excuse to annex the Sudetenland. Eighty years later, the comment continues to irritate the Czechs, in large part because it remains accurate for much of the Anglophone world. Bookstore shelves groan with histories of England, France, Germany, and other familiar countries of Western Europe, and there are always plenty of histories of Russia nearby. But there are very few, if any, on the lands in between, aside from histories of the horrific fighting in the Second World War. The Western world maintains an incurious attitude about "Eastern Europe" that would have been foreign to Europeans of the fourteenth- and fifteenth-centuries. Then, the Kingdom of Poland and Lithuania was the most powerful in Europe, the Holy Roman Empire stretched from the Low Countries to Hungary, and Prague was its Second City. Bohemia was an important, centrally located kingdom within the Empire, a midpoint between German- and French-speaking lands on the West, and Hungarian- and Slavic-speaking lands on the East.

Bohemia was torn apart by the Hussite phenomenon between 1419 and 1435, and all of Europe reacted with horror as its violence spread into Bavaria, Silesia, Moravia, and the Baltic states. Such violence usually accompanied wars between crowns or powerful lords, but here it was waged by lesser nobles, theologians, and commoners. In many histories of the Hussites, it has been common to push aside the theological justifications for the fighting as secondary, masking nationalist or economic issues that are the "real movers" in politics. This is due to the secularism that continues to define Western civilization, separating it from societies in which religion continues to dominate, notably the Muslim world. It is almost impossible to believe that common people would take up farm implements to meet mounted armoured knights in combat for access to the consecrated wine of the Eucharist. Surely there was more at stake than this?

This history, the briefest of overviews of the Hussites, is designed to show why theology was so important to all involved. Its two main chapters are about the events that occurred between 1419 and 1435, the period of main hostilities, and the ideas that animated the behaviour of the Hussites and their opponents. As in the Muslim world today, theology and politics are inextricably connected, and the final chapter will show how this connection has gradually been recovered in contemporary history. The two main parties in the Hussite movement, Prague and Tábor, regularly met in acrimonious attempts to iron out theological differences. The violence only came to an end when Prague recognized that Tábor's refusal to compromise on theological issues was becoming insuperable. Other historians have cast this story in terms of Czech nationalism, or as a class struggle between the city bourgeois and the rural proletariat, or as the labour pains for the events that would produce the Protestant Reformation. These are all anachronisms, histories describing events of the fifteenth century in terms defined in the nineteenth century. The tendency among scholars and historians of the post-Soviet era has been to pay much more attention to the theology behind Hussitism, an approach that this work will attempt to reflect.

The great barrier to the study of the Hussites continues to be the lack of availability of instruction in the Czech language. As will become clear, the great renaissance of the Czech language and culture of the mid-nineteenth century centred on the Hussites, and especially Jan Hus himself, as the historical moment of Czech self-definition. The scholarship on the Hussite period is vast, and encompasses theology, politics, social history, church–state relations, economics, and has led to a wealth of editions of Hussite works—all in Czech. At a recent conference, some Anglophone scholars referred to the Hussite period as a veritable goldmine, rich with opportunities for groundbreaking work, within earshot of some Czech scholars, who were understandably nonplussed. On the other hand, Czech scholars continue to produce original and often brilliant scholarship in a language to which access remains notably difficult. Additionally, they have been heard to grumble that nobody who is not a Czech can really understand the Hussite movement, an odd sentiment for citizens of a country with the greatest proportion of atheists in the world. One might as easily wonder how anyone who is not a medieval priest can possibly understand medieval theology. The divisions that separated Bohemia from the West so dramatically as to give rise to Chamberlain's question continue to bedevil Hussite scholarship.

There is a very broad range of subjects relevant to the study of the Hussites that do not appear in this narrative. These include the development of vernacular Hussite litera-ture, hymnody, and litugy, the impact of the Hussites on con-temporary theological discourse at the church councils of Kon-stanz and Basel, and in universities across Europe, the rich cultural and literary interplay between England and Bohemia, the economic relation of towns, villages, and manor farms in Bohemia, the relation of the kingdom of Bohemia to the rest of the Holy Roman Empire, and the manifold repercussions of the papal schism. I say nothing of religious iconography and Hus-site iconoclasm, the role of Hus in the Reformation, and very little of hostile contemporary narratives, such as that of Aeneas Silvius Piccolomini, regarding the Hussites. Recent important contributions to these topics have enriched contemporary scholarship.[1] Readers may also be surprised to find Jan Hus playing a much smaller role in this narrative than is usual. This is because his later reputation has been used to elevate him above his contemporaries and successors with a hagiographic awe. More able theologians like Jakoubek and Rokycana remain in the shadows. One would think that it took the Bohemian reform movement four years to recover from his death before its leaders could work up their spirits to stage the Defenestration. His works continue to be read as though they alone encapsulate the Hussite theology, despite his having said almost nothing about utraquism (congregants taking Communion in both kinds, bread and wine, instead of bread alone), and the fact that most of what he had said on other topics had already been said by earlier Bohemian theologians like Matěj of Janov.

I am grateful to a number of scholars for their support and help with this project, whether intentional or accidental. These include Thomas Fudge, František Šmahel, Peter Morée, Pavel Soukup, Michael van Dussen, Philip Haberkern, Martin Dekarli, Ivan Mueller, Ota Pavlicek, David Holeton, Ždanek David, Ian Levy, Fiona Somerset, Pavlina Cermanová, and Simon Forde. I am especially indebted to the late Howard Kaminsky, who gave me a wealth of literature to encourage my study of the Hussites, and to Vilém Herold, who invited me to work on his edition of Wyclif's *De Ideis*. I am also indebted to Zdeněk Vybiral and the curators of the Hussite Museum in Tábor, who generously provided me with the invaluable volumes of *Husitský Tábor*, and to the many scholars who regularly participate in the biennial "Bohemian Reformation and Religious Practice" conferences. The mistakes, inaccuracies, and infuriating conclusions contained herein are all my own.

*Žádám ty, kteři vy, aby mi odpustili a udělat lépe, než jsem udělal.*

────────────

**I** See Katarina Horničkova and Michal Sronek, *From Hus to Luther: Visual Culture in the Bohemian Reformation, 1380–1620* (Turnhout: Brepols, 2017), and Phillip Haberkern, *Patron Saint and Prophet: Jan Hus in the Bohemian and German Reformation* (Oxford: Oxford University Press, 2016).

## Leading Figures in the Hussite History

| | | |
|---|---|---|
| Adalbert Ranconis | d. 1388 | Theologian, trained in Paris |
| Aleš Vřeštovský | d. 1442 | Orebite commander |
| Ambrož Hradecký | d. 1439 | Priest, leader of Orebites |
| Čapek of Sany | d. 1455 | Orebite commander |
| Čenek of Vartenberk | d. 1425 | Burgrave of Prague, commander of Royalist forces |
| Charles IV | d. 1378 | Holy Roman Emperor, father of Václav and Sigismund |
| Diviš Bořek | d. 1438 | Moderate Hussite general |
| Jakoubek Stříbro | d. 1429 | Theologian, mediated between conservative Prague and Tábor |
| Jan Hus | d. 1415 | Theologian, preacher, condemned and killed at Konstanz |
| Jan Jensteyn | d. 1409 | Archbishop of Prague, 1379–1396 |
| Jan Milíč of Kromeřiž | d. 1374 | Preacher, model for Hussite ideal priest |
| Jan Papošek of Soběslav | d. 1454 | Scholar, later opponent of Hussites |
| Jan Přibram | d. 1448 | Theologian, conservative Prague master |
| Jan Rohač of Dubá | d. 1437 | Orebite general, last military leader of Tábor |
| Jan Rokycana | d. 1471 | Theologian, moderate Prague Master, Archbishop of Prague |
| Jan Želivský | d. 1422 | Preacher, attempted Táborite coup in Prague |
| Jan Žižka of Trochno | d. 1425 | Táborite general |
| Jerome of Prague | d. 1415 | Theologian, influential associate of Hus |
| Jiři Poděbradý | d. 1471 | King of Bohemia, the "Hussite King" |
| John Wyclif | d. 1384 | English theologian, condemned for heresy |

## Leading Figures in the Hussite History *(cont.)*

| | | |
|---|---|---|
| Konrad Waldhauser | d. 1369 | Austrian priest, influential in mid-fourteenth-century Bohemia |
| Laurence of Březová | d. 1437 | Author of *Hussite Chronicle* |
| Luke of Prague | d. 1511 | Leader of *Unitas fratrum* |
| Menhart of Hradec | d. 1449 | Moderate Hussite noble |
| Petr Chelčický | d. 1460 | Vernacular theologian, radical pacifist–anarchist |
| Peter Payne | d. 1455 | English theologian, diplomat, prominent at Council of Basel |
| Prokop Holý | d. 1435 | Hussite general, heir to Žižka legacy |
| Matěj of Janov | d. 1393 | Theologian, influential for Hussite theology |
| Nicholas "Biskupec" of Pehlřimov | d. 1452 | Táborite theologian |
| Nicholas of Dresden | d. 1417/19 | German theologian, originated Utraquist position with Jakoubek |
| Sigismund of Luxembourg | d. 1437 | Holy Roman Emperor, later King of Bohemia |
| Sigismund Korybut | d. 1435 | Polish aristocrat, claimed Bohemian throne |
| Stanislaus of Znojmo | d. 1414 | Wycliffite theologian, later opponent of Hus |
| Stepan Páleč | d. 1424 | Wycliffite theologian, later opponent of Hus |
| Tomáš Stítný | d. 1401/09 | Vernacular theologian, influential on Hussite reform |
| Václav IV | d. 1412 | otherwise known as Wenceslas IV, King of Bohemia |
| Václav Koranda | d. 1453 | Táborite theologian |
| Zbyněk Zajic | d. 1411 | Archbishop of Prague, 1403–1411 |

Chapter 1

# Hussite Theologians

The Hussite movement was defined by its theology in a way difficult for modern, or postmodern, readers to understand. The 1986 movie *The Name of the Rose*, based on Umberto Eco's (strangely bestselling) novel, featured a scene in which a roomful of angry Franciscans, Benedictines, Dominicans, and high ranking bishops and a cardinal had gathered to resolve a problem that had caused the church to reach a point of actually persecuting a minority of Franciscan friars. The debate, it was announced in dead seriousness, was whether Christ and His disciples did, or did not, own the purse that contained their pooled meagre resources. The effect in the movie is to cause incredulity in the audience. *This* was what had led to political unrest, the detective work of Inquisitors, and the prospect of accusations of heresy? But Eco's portrayal of the argument behind the Franciscan Poverty controversy was fairly accurate: some friars were indeed willing to go to the stake rather than admit that the early church had truck with property ownership. Our secular society's departure from the medieval world is so profound as to make it difficult to believe that people would risk their lives on such apparently trivial concerns. With the Hussites, the issue uniting the otherwise fractious alliance of Tábor and Prague was agreement that the standing church practice of not offering the consecrated wine to the laity was so serious as to merit taking up arms. In this chapter, I will describe the reasoning, and the consequent debates on this and other subjects that animated Hussitism.

The Four Articles of Prague of 1421 will serve as a general organizing point, because they contained the core of what the Hussites believed should define a Christian society. Three of these four articles were already being discussed in Prague in 1388, when Wyclif's works began to appear there. The fourth, the issue of lay access to the chalice, arose shortly after Jan Hus left Prague for his fateful trip to Konstanz. We will survey a broad range of thinkers, who represent an equally broad range of theological positions. Questions of the nature of the church, the relation of ecclesiastical to scriptural authority, the immediacy of the Apocalypse and the threat of Antichrist, of how to worship, how to love God and love one's neighbour, and how to self-identify as a Christian, all were related to these Articles in a program of reform that had been causing trouble when Jan Hus was still a young man in Husinec. So we will begin by surveying the Bohemian reform movement before Hus appeared, with the sermons of Jan Milíč, and the theology of Matěj of Janov, as well as the ideas of John Wyclif as they were received in Prague in the 1390s. From there, we will proceed roughly chronologically. The main figures during the first years of the Hussite movement were Jan Hus, Jerome of Prague, Jakoubek Stříbro, and Nicholas of Dresden. Hus is by far the most famous of these, but as I will show, he was not the leader of the early Hussites. That honour went to Jakoubek, who was generally recognized as such until his death in 1429. Next, we will consider the two factions that defined Hussitism, namely the Prague party led by Jan Rokycana and Jan Příbram, and the Tábor party led by Mikulaš Biskupec, and partially abetted by Peter Payne. Hussite internal relations were very strongly identified by the constant bickering between these two parties, and the end of the hostilities in 1435 came about very much because Tabor finally became too intractable for Prague. Our last figure has a place of his own for two reasons. While a contemporary of these figures, and likely well known to most of them, Petr Chelčický had a completely different version of the reform that should define Bohemian Christianity. Biskupec was known to meet with him from time to time, and there is evidence that Petr had known

Jakoubek, but he was a radical pacifist, and so *vox clamantis in deserto* (a "voice crying in the wilderness") during the violent decades of the Hussite war. Petr was very important for the continuation of Hussitism into early Modernity, though, because of the role he would play in formulating what would become the Moravian theology.

The figures and arguments defining Hussite theology are closely related to the historical narrative that follows in Chapter 2. To assist the reader threading a path through the many names of theologians, nobles, diplomats, and warriors that define the narrative, I have included for guidance a *Dramatis Personae* at the end of the introduction.

## The Four Articles

The Eucharist was at the centre of late medieval Latin Christianity. Of the seven sacraments by which the believing Christian could be assured of receiving the grace necessary for salvation, the sacrament of the altar had pride of place. In 1215, Innocent III had declared that the bread and wine were transformed into the real body and blood of Christ while retaining their former appearances, a doctrine that soon became known as transubstantiation. Such was the power of the transubstantiated bread that simply seeing it held aloft was regarded as sufficient for reception of its salvific properties. Stories arose about miracles arising from physical contact with the sacred body and blood, as did horrific accusations against Jews for supposedly stealing the elements and somehow torturing them. Theologians devoted considerable attention to the sacrament when completing a commentary on the *Sentences* of Peter Lombard, a necessary condition for receiving the doctoral degree. In time, arguments about how transubstantiation took place became extraordinarily complex and abstract, leading some theologians to begin to question the assumption that the logic of theology and the logic of the physical world were commensurate.

When a group of Bohemian nobles gathered in June 1420, a year after the defenestration in Prague that launched the

Hussite movement, they published a list of four specific ideals that all had agreed defined the movement. Foremost among these four articles of Prague was the Utraquist demand, namely that the laity be allowed to receive both (*utraque*) consecrated bread and wine, rather than the bread alone, which had long been the custom. Utraquism was peculiar to the Hussite movement, even if individual Hussites disagreed bitterly about other aspects of sacramental theology. In time, the symbol of the chalice used to administer the consecrated wine symbolized the Hussites, flying on their banners and emblazoned on their pavises (the large shield protecting Hussite gunners and crossbowmen). The orthodox position of concomitance, that Christ is fully present in both consecrated elements, allows the communicant to receive the full benefits of the sacrament by consuming one of the elements, which the Utraquist position cast into doubt. While it was, and is, not heretical for a Roman Catholic to receive both consecrated elements, it was, and is, heresy to reject concomitance, as the Hussites did. Some Hussites went much farther. They followed John Wyclif, the Oxford theologian who had been condemned for heresy for his rejection of transubstantiation. Wyclif had argued that the doctrine simply was not possible according to Aristotle's physics, and after struggling to come up with an explanation for the miraculous transformation, declared that the bread and wine remained in the consecrated elements, a position that came to be known as "remanentist." While remanentism had been in the air in Prague after Wyclf's works had become popular there in the 1390s and 1400s, Hus had carefully avoided denying transubstantiation. His colleague, Jakoubek of Stříbro, who would assume the mantle of the movement's leading theologian after Hus's death, advocated the remanentist position, as did the leader of the Táborite camp, Nicholas Biskupec, but the later, more moderate Prague Hussites, notably Jan Rokycana and Jan Přibram defended transubstantiation.

The three other Articles of Prague were more familiar demands that had been being made over the past two hundred years. Two were expressly about the clergy. First, the clergy should be constrained to lives exemplary of the moral purity of Christ and the apostles, which was widely assumed to entail rejection of all civil lordship and power. Second, the clergy should not be constrained in preaching and teaching the Scriptures by any ecclesiastical authority and should be free to preach in the vernacular. In themselves, these were not surprising demands; the issue of clerical ownership had come up in the Franciscan poverty controversy at the end of the thirteenth century, and the demands for the improvement of the morals of the clergy had been common throughout the Christian world since the Fourth Lateran Council in 1215. Further, the preaching friars had been giving sermons in the vernacular without supervision by local bishops since their foundation in the thirteenth century. The problems arose in the details. The Hussites were disposed to allowing the secular, civil authorities to divest the clergy of their property and political power. This had been the position articulated by John Wyclif, which had been declared heretical both in London (1382) and in Avignon (1384). Again, the Hussites were disposed to local priests being free to preach as they felt called, without episcopal supervision, another position supported by Wyclif that had already been condemned.

The fourth article was that mortal sins should be publicly corrected, so that the Bohemian nation could more completely live in Christian harmony and obedience. This demand immediately leads to several serious questions: who decides which sins ought to be publicly punished, who carries out the punishment, and what body of law takes precedence in cases where the guilty party has broken no civil law? It was tied to widespread desires to enforce Christian moral laws, but suggests the subversion of civil law to an inchoate Christian morality that would lead to two disparate Hussite conceptions of society: the strictly regulated, proto-fundamentalist society of Tábor, and the recognizably moderate Christian monarchy of the Prague masters. While Wyclif had advocated for a position commensurate with the Prague masters, he had not made public punishment of mortal sins a main plank in his intellectual platform; his interest was in the royal reformation of the church, and he perceived the sermon as a more important corrective than public punishment.

How much did these four articles rely upon Jan Hus? It is reasonable to assume that the Hussites were so named because they had adopted the teachings and ideas of Hus, but this is not altogether accurate. First, Hus did not originate the Utraquist position; Jakoubek and Nicholas of Dresden were behind it, and Hus only made brief comment in favour of it before he left for Konstanz. During his trial, his prosecutors made much of condemning utraquism, which Hus regarded as unreasonable and contrary to the spirit of early Christianity, but that is the extent of his advocacy for the most important theological aspect of the Hussite movement. The articles regarding clerical morality and preaching appear throughout Hus's writings, as they do in the works of a great many other late medieval thinkers. Their formulation is not notably inspired by anything unique to Hus. Finally, evidence for the fourth can be found in Hus's *De ecclesia* chap. 23, but the public correction he has in mind is for priests not suited to preaching the gospels. In his later work, *De sufficiencia legis Christi*, he argues that Christ's law as expressed in Scripture is all that is needed for governing the church, but adds that canon and civil law that is in agreement with Christ's law is useful for governance in human society as well. While this is consonant with the later, more moderate Prague masters' interpretation of this fourth article, it is difficult to conceive this brief comment being taken as the basis for one of four articles fundamental to the movement.

If the Four Articles do not spring fully formed from Hus's works, where did the assembled nobles get them? To address this, we must first do three things. We will need to discuss the reformative ideals percolating in Bohemian culture when Hus was still a boy. Second, because Wyclif has been so long connected with the Hussite movement, we will develop a picture of how much of a hand Wyclif's writings had in the development of the Hussite theology. Third, we will need to examine two thinkers in particular: Jan Hus, and the real theological mind behind the birth of Hussitism, Jakoubek. With these addressed, we should then follow the development of the two duelling Hussite theological visions, from Prague in 1420 to Lipany in 1434 (when the Hussite war with the Emperor ended), and beyond.

## Before Hus: Milíč, Matěj, and Wyclif

Czechs had been thinking about the need for church reform throughout the fourteenth century. The Waldensian movement had gained some traction in Bohemia, and the Czech-born Emperor Charles IV had great interest in building up the faith in his native land. The first important figure for understanding the rise of Hussitism, though, was Jan Milíč of Kroměříž, a charismatic preacher and minister to the poor who was active in Prague in the 1360s and 70s. Milíč was born near Zlín in Moravia in the early part of the fourteenth century, ordained in 1348 in the diocese of Olomouc, and moved to Prague in the late 1350s. He served in the chancery of Charles IV, and travelled with the emperor to Wrocław and Nürnberg. He moved to work in the Prague curia in 1362, where his talents brought him the office of archdeacon the next year. His responsibilities involved evaluating the moral and doctrinal state of the clergy in the diocese, which experience appears to have had great effect on him. He also encountered the preaching of Konrad Waldhauser, an Austrian priest Charles had brought to Prague to instil an evangelical spirit among his clergy. These two experiences changed him, instilling a powerful feeling of the need for preaching and ministering to the poor, which he began in the Lesser Town area of Prague in 1364. He began collecting his sermons around this time in the postil *Abortivus*, which presents a vision of society suffering from moral collapse, a church infected with corrupt clergy and hypocritical bishops, and the hand of antichrist increasingly gaining control of the Christian world. Milíč learned of the reformative interests of Urban V, who wanted to restore the papal see to Rome from Avignon, and decided to travel there to present his ideas to the pontiff. He arrived before Urban V did, and announced his intention to preach in St. Peter's, which quickly landed him in prison. The inquisitors were not impressed with the dark vision of his sermons, so he composed a small treatise, *Libellus de Antichristo*, while in prison in 1367. When Urban arrived, Milíč was released and appears to have had an amicable meeting with the pope. He returned to Prague and continued to develop a reputation as a firebrand preacher. After another visit with Urban in 1369, he returned to Prague and assumed the mantle of the recently deceased Waldhauser. He became increasingly respected as an inspiring preacher and an example of a life absolutely given over to Christ. In the early 1370s, he began to focus his attentions on the moral reformation of poor women and managed to convert two hundred prostitutes in Prague's red-light district, known as Venice. He organized a lay piety community evocative of a beguinage there, renaming the district Jerusalem.

This crossed the line for several priests and friars in Prague, who accused him of setting up his own mini-diocese in Jerusalem. Milíč was tried and compelled to abandon his ministry there, and he decided to appeal to the pope. But Urban had died, and Gregory XI was now pope in Avignon. Gregory was deeply suspicious of Milíč and ordered him to appear at the papal court in 1374. Milíč travelled there and was examined by the Augustinian friar Johannes Klenkok. Klenkok, a noted conservative theologian, found Milíč to be perfectly orthodox, and in short order, Milíč was invited to preach before the pope. Soon after his sermon on Pentecost, he died in Avignon, far from home, but vindicated.

Other priests in Prague had noticed Milíč as well. The Theology Faculty at Charles University had been dominated by Germans since the University's founding in 1348. They taught the dominant theological systems of the period, the *moderni* theology of the Ockhamists, and the more conservative Aristotelian syntheses of Thomism and Scotism. When enough Czech students had established themselves there, a contingent went to Paris to form the base for a Czech theological faculty. There they encountered the Latin Neoplatonic thought that had defined twelfth-century philosophical theology before Aristotle's thought was fully recovered. They admired the Platonism of the Victorine thinkers, William de Conches and Anselm, and brought this strong realism back to Prague. Of these newly Platonized Bohemians, Adalbert Ranconis and Matěj of Janov were the leaders. Adalbert went on to lead the Czech students into adopting a Neoplatonist approach that was the antithesis of the *moderni* and the Aristotelian syntheses, while Matěj served in the diocesan seat at St. Vitus Cathedral. Another figure, a layman named Tomáš Štítný, developed a taste for a mystic theology similar to what the Czechs brought with them from Paris. He also had a great interest in preparing devotional and educational treatises in Czech for the laity, and he became a key figure in the 1360s and 70s in the growing nativist theological movement.

The most important figure, though, was Matěj of Janov. He composed an extensive collection of treatises explaining how a turn back to the simple purity of the early church would restore Christendom in time for the swiftly approaching Last Days. His *Regulae Veteri et Novi Testamentum*, a collection of five treatises in which the Christian need for daily Eucharist predominates, can almost appear to be a blueprint for the Hussite movement. Matěj was reprimanded for his ideas at the Prague Synod of 1389, and compelled to recant for his criticisms of the clergy and the papacy. While he never gained the academic notoriety that later Bohemian reformers would, remaining as canon at Prague cathedral until his death in 1394, his *Regulae* contains the seeds for the Four Articles that would define the movement.

The *Regulae* is formidably dense, repetitive, and curiously organized. The whole of it has been published, much of it in a set of volumes edited by Vlastimíl Kybal in the early decades of the twentieth century, and the last volume by Jana Nechutová in 1993. There are seventeen rules Matěj describes for the Christian life, understood in the broadest sense possible, including both individual life, clerical morality, and church governance. The first set of eight rules are based in the Old Testament; four for recognizing false prophets, and four for overcoming them through daily universal participation in the sacrament of Eucharist. The second set of eight rules are based in the New Testament; four for recognizing hypocrisy in ministers and preachers, and four for the clergy to use in overcoming hypocrisy and living a life given over to Christ. The remaining law is the Eternal Law of God, the fundamental Truth of creation binding it to the Creator's will. Matěj begins describing this law in recognizably Neoplatonic terms, equating this Law with the Word of God, the incarnation of which established Christ's mystical body on earth. The *corpus mysticum* was a term that had been used to refer to the Eucharist until the thirteenth century, when it gradually began to be used instead to refer to the church as Christ's body on earth. Matěj perceived the term to refer to both at once, thus understanding that the church considered as the body of faithful Christians making up Christ's earthly body must be nourished daily by the body and blood Christ offers in the sacrament of Eucharist.

The remaining books of the *Regulae* pursue the implications of this understanding of the *corpus mysticum* for the church in the world. By the time Matěj wrote, the church was split in half by the Western Schism, with an Italian pope in Rome, and a French pope in Avignon. Europe was divided between the two, and Matěj saw the strain of this division was tearing the body apart. The direct result, Matěj argued, was the immediate reality of antichrist dominating Christ's body on earth. His treatise on antichrist, which Bernard McGinn describes as among the longest such in medieval literature, argues that antichrist is already present throughout the church, wherever clergy are using their office to secure worldly power and wealth instead of serving the laity. Any pope, any emperor, anyone in power whatsoever who contributes to this is antichrist. The hallmark of antichrist, Matěj explains, is clerical hypocrisy, so the duty of the preacher is to champion the life and teachings of Christ in opposing it. Hence, the eight rules described at the work's beginning provide the structure for becoming actively engaged in combatting antichrist. The preacher and his faithful flock can only do this supplemented by grace, which is provided by daily

Eucharist. Only through scripturally sound preaching by a soul who has devoted his entire life to Christ, and through the daily celebration of Christ's sacrifice, can antichrist be overcome and the body of Christ be prepared for Christ's return.

The base for three of the four Articles of Prague is found in Matěj. Contained within Matěj's argument is a strident call for punishment of clergy who continue to indulge in mortal sin to illustrate the great danger that a preacher living a faithless life poses to the laity, the demand that all clergy surrender their mundane wealth, power, and privilege in their dedication of themselves to a life imitating the purity of the apostles, and the continued call for regular preaching of the Christian life and the demands it makes on individual Christians. However, with regard to utraquism, Matěj does not expressly call for daily consumption of both consecrated elements of the Eucharist; he says that the laity must consume the consecrated bread daily but does not expressly mention lay consumption of the consecrated wine.

How widely was Matěj read after his death? The manuscript evidence shows numerous codices remaining containing one or several books of the *Regulae*, with only one part of one book apparently lost for good. R. R. Betts, the first Anglophone scholar to recognize the significance of Matěj's thought for the Hussite movement, argues, following F. M. Bartoš, that Hus must have been deeply familiar with Matěj, and Jakoubek openly cites long passages from the *Regulae* throughout his works.

Matěj included a hagiographical biography of Milíč in the section of the *Regulae* where he describes the building body of evidence for antichrist's threat to society. This section, the last part of his *De Antichristo*, the heart of the *Regulae*, begins with Matěj citing the whole of William of St. Amour's *De periculis novissimorum temporum*, a famous description of the part the church is playing in the coming of the End Times. Next, Matěj describes how theologians have been awakening to this threat, finishing with a biography of Milíč and the whole of Milíč's *Libellus*. Matěj very obviously considers Milíč to have lived the ideal life of the preacher of the gospel, giving his all to a life in Christ's service, fearlessly exposing the foul hypocrisy that infects the body of Christ, and bravely facing prison and even death in preaching the gospels. Bett's comments on the startling correspondence of Hus's career as preacher and reformer to the blueprint Matěj provides in his description of ministry in the *Regulae*. We will return to this shortly.

At the bottom of the first page of one manuscript of the *Regulae* there is a note saying "Tractatus of John Wikleff the heretic: Read this with care, lest you fall into a deathly trap," which is crossed out by another hand, and replaced by "This tractatus is by Master Matthew of Paris, so read this with care, lest you fall into error." This nicely summarizes the predicament historians of the Hussites face. Readers have been finding things in Hussite writings that seem to come from Wyclif, but really come from Matěj. In part this is thanks to some very sloppy scholarship by a noted church historian of the nineteenth century, Johann Loserth, whose *Wyclif und Hus* argued that Hus simply plagiarized his thought from Wyclif. In part this is understandable, given the many instances in which Hus actually does use several paragraphs of Wyclif's work in his own arguments. But to conclude that all of Hus's program derives from Wyclif is premature. One of Loserth's students, Mathilde Uhlirz, made a similar claim about the originality of the Four Articles, and her brief monograph was met with a vituperative response by Václav Novotný, whose blistering contempt justly characterizes Czech attitudes towards this line of reasoning. The question naturally follows, though: how much did Wyclif contribute to the Hussite theology?

John Wyclif (d. 1384) was Oxford University's greatest thinker in the second half of the fourteenth century, formulating a philosophical system incorporating the ontological realism of Giles of Rome and Walter Burley into a sophisticated logic and semantics influenced by Ockhamist *moderni* like Adam Wodeham. He appears to have reworked his *Sentences* commentary into a series of thirteen treatises, making up his *Summa theologie*, describing the metaphysics of God and creation. He also composed logical treatises in which he interwove questions of traditional scholastic logic with his metaphysics, and several other shorter philosophical treatises. Further, he developed a pastoral theology designed to compete against the friars' preaching, with a homiletic guide, a carefully described hermeneutic of Scripture, a set of Latin sermons, commentaries on the decalogue (Ten Commandments), and on several important sections of the gospels. He is best remembered, though, for his incendiary critiques of the church and its practices. His treatises on dominion emphasize a concept deriving from the traditional idea that all earthly power comes from God, that of grace-founded dominion. By his reasoning, the only just lordship in human society is exercised by those God has chosen and endowed with grace to serve as stewards of God's creation. He holds both sacred and secular lords to this standard, arguing that individuals occupying exalted office in state or in the church who do not embody the moral standards of the gospels are not fit to hold those offices. God will take care of evil kings and civil lords, he says, but it is the civil lord's duty to take care of errant clergy. So the best thing for present society, Wyclif concludes, is for the king to divest the church of all its wealth and political power, and to compel bishops and popes to live ascetic lives of holiness and continued prayer.

The justification for this royal reform is that God eternally understands the membership of the Church to be the body of the Elect, and civil lords are responsible for the safekeeping of that body. If ordained priests and bishops in that body are behaving evilly, the civil lords are duty bound to protect the body by correcting them. Wyclif has treatises outlining the true nature of the papacy, the evils of simony, apostasy, and blasphemy, and the threat posed the church by "private religions," or the friars. The most dangerous of Wyclif's writings, though, were his thoughts on the Eucharist. Wyclif struggled mightily to align the physics of transubstantiation with Aristotelian thought, and concluded that the transformation that describes the essence of the sacrament's nature is not only physically impossible, but contrary to the divine nature. He reduces the doctrine of transubstantiation to a set of mutually exclusive ideas, but in the end, was unable to provide an alternative explanation of what happens when the bread and wine are consecrated. At best, he says that Christ is really present in the consecrated elements, but that the bread and wine remain in their essence still present after the consecration.

Wyclif knew that his thought was complicated and difficult for non-theologians to understand, so he composed two works designed for generally educated priests and lay people, the *Dyalogus* and *Trialogus*. *Dyalogus*, a dialogue between "Truth" and "Lying," covering Wyclif's thought on the church, the papacy, the Eucharist, and the friars, was very popular in Bohemia, with eighteen remaining manuscripts in Bohemian hands. The *Trialogus* is much longer, covering most of what is included in the *Sentences* of Peter Lombard, the scholastic compendium of issues in Christian theology. As its name suggests, it is a three-way dialogue between Wyclif, a wise young student, and a lying friar, and in addition to the standard subjects of a *Sentences* commentary, it contains all of what is included in the *Dyalogus* as a *supplementum*. Hus was so taken by the *Trialogus* that he translated it into Czech, but this appears to have been lost; Jakoubek's Czech translation of the *Dyalogus* remains, though, and was edited in 1909.

When Wyclif's works arrived in Prague in the 1380s, his philosophical theology, the treatises of the *Summa de ente*, caused the most stir. They provided the Bohemian theological students the philosophical machinery with which to develop their extant generally Neoplatonist ontology into a sophisticated alternative to the theology of the German masters. Soon, the Bohemian nation in the Charles University faculty of theology were championing Wyclif's theories of divine ideas and universals. Foremost among them was Stanislaus of Znojmo (d. 1414), whose philosophical abilities rivalled those of any of the German faculty. Stanislaus developed a commentary on Wyclif's philosophy that was so evocative of Wyclif's thought that editors of the nineteenth-century Wyclif Society published Stanislaus's *De universalibus* as the work of Wyclif. For close to twenty-five years, Wycliffism was extremely popular at Charles University. As Wyclif's more dangerous reformative thought began to gain a foothold among the Bohemian students, though, the masters of the university and the archbishop of Prague began to discourage Wycliffism. Between 1403 and 1409, Wycliffism became increasingly associated with heresy, just as students like Jerome of Prague, Jan Hus, and Jakoubek of Stříbro began to articulate their own uniquely Bohemian Wycliffism. Stanislaus of Znojmo and Stephan Páleč were invited to Rome to explore their errors, and when they returned in 1409, they were zealous in their opposition to the Wycliffism of their students. Stanislaus died before matters would come to a head at the Council in Konstanz, but Páleč would play a role in Hus's eventual fate.

## Hus, Jerome, Jakoubek, and Nicholas of Dresden

A number of Bohemian theology students were important advocates of Wyclif, but the most important of them were Jan Hus, Jerome of Prague, and Jakoubek of Stříbro. While Hus is the movement's namesake, Jerome was arguably as important as Hus in the years before 1415, while Jakoubek, who died in 1425, was the real theological voice of Hussitism. Hus, from the town of Husinec in Bohemia (the name means "goose") enrolled at Charles University in 1390, where he studied Wyclif's thought and was ordained to the priesthood in 1400. He quickly gained a reputation for preaching in both Latin and Czech, and was assigned to Bethlehem chapel in Prague's Old Town in 1402. Bethlehem chapel was so named because it was close by Milíč's "Jerusalem," and was designated in 1391 as the primary location in Prague for preaching in Czech. Hus continued his theological studies throughout the decade, completing his *Sentences* commentary in 1409. At this point, Wycliffism was increasingly being regarded as heretical, and the archbishop of Prague was actively opposed to it. Hus's *Sentences* commentary appears to be absolutely without any heretical ideas, so has been dismissed as theologically uninteresting, but he champions Wyclif's metaphysics in subtle ways, enough to identify his inclinations but not enough to endanger himself. 1409 was an important year for Hus; he was elected rector of Charles University, and he used this influential position to urge King Wenceslas, Charles IV's son, to equalize the voting rights in the theological faculty at the university. The arrangement was that the Saxons, the Bavarians, the Poles, and the Czechs were equal, but the reality was that the first three faculties all voted in a bloc. Wenceslas ordained that the three "German" nations would have only one vote in total, and the Czechs would have one, thereby making the Czechs more powerful than the other three faculties. This decree, made in the nearby mining town of Kutná Hora, so incensed the "Germans" that they left Prague en masse and founded the University of Leipzig. 1409 also saw the nascent Czech reform movement crystallize around Hus, thanks to his preaching notoriety (Wenceslas's Queen Sophie was a fan) and his status in the university. The next year found Hus directly opposed to Archbishop Zbyněk of Prague, whose early permissiveness toward Wycliffism had hardened into active opposition. Encouraged by Alexander V, recently appointed pope at the Council of Pisa in hopes of resolving the Western Schism, Zbyněk decreed a complete ban of all study of Wyclif's works. Hus and his associates openly opposed the archbishop, preaching against his authority in Bethlehem chapel and publicly defending Wyclif's works. In 1411, the curial court in Prague demanded that Hus appear, to explain himself, which Hus refused to do. He was anathematized in March, which meant that he was forbidden from executing his priestly office, and that any faithful Christian was bound to avoid him at all costs.

Hus continued in his preaching against Zbyněk, all of the popes, and the abuses of the clergy in the face of diocesan opposition. When Zbyněk suddenly died in September 1411, Hus concentrated his efforts against the corrupt papacy. Pope Alexander V died and was followed by John XXIII, who immediately launched an ambitious campaign of selling indulgences in Prague, giving Hus and his followers more fodder for their preaching. By the end of 1412, Hus could no longer safely remain in Prague, and went into exile in southern Bohemia.

There his reputation as a preacher and reformer grew, and his outdoor sermons were said to draw thousands. While in exile at Kozí Hradek in southern Bohemia, Hus wrote some of his most important works. Following the example of Tomáš Štítný, he wrote several works summarizing his understanding of the Christian life for the laity, including the *Výklad véry* (an exposition of the faith), and one especially for lay women, *Dcerka* (Daughter). His most important Latin work, *De ecclesia*, was the product of his stay in 1413 at Kozí Hradek. Hostility between Hus's reform party and the archdiocese and Rome continued to build, leading to a riot in which three young men were killed by city authorities.

Emperor Sigismund, the brother of King Wenceslas, was growing concerned for Bohemia, and decided that the best way of resolving things was to have Hus come to the Ecumenical Council being held in Konstanz. The alert reader will note that there had been councils in Pisa and Rome within the past three years already; why another council? This was the period of the conciliarist movement, when theologians were carefully rethinking the papacy, weakened by the Western Schism and notoriously open to abuses. Pierre d'Ailly and Jean Gerson were the two primary figures arguing for a restructuring of authority in the church, with the lion's share of responsibility being taken from the papacy and to be placed in the hands of an ecumenical council of bishops. What better proof could they offer for the reasonability of such an arrangement then demonstrating that they could handle the threat Hus and his movement posed to the internal security of the church?

Things did not go as planned when Hus travelled to Konstanz in 1414. He was immediately imprisoned, despite the promise of safe conduct made by Sigismund (which admittedly had not been issued until after he had arrived). Hus had imagined that he would present his views to a roomful of rational bishops and doctors of the church, who would carefully consider his arguments, perhaps the way Alexander IV had done with Milíč. Instead, he was imprisoned in a dark cell, and eventually accused of forty heretical errors. These errors boil down to four topics. First, Hus was accused of arguing that the Church was only the congregation of the eternally predestined Elect, and that the foreknown (the damned) have never been part of Christ's body on earth. Second, he was accused of Donatism, namely the position that priests living immorally so pollute their office as to render them ineffective ministers of the sacraments. Third, he was accused of having proclaimed the papacy to be a Caesarean invention, designed to attain and maintain political power. The true pope was only knowable through divine revelation, not through the election of the cardinals, and that the present popes are little more than devils and robbers. Finally, he was accused of arguing that the ecclesiastical hierarchy exists merely to propagate the material power and wealth of the church, and that its habit of excommunication was theologically meaningless. Hus refused to recant these positions, flatly stating that he was not guilty of holding them, and that no one but Christ was authorized to judge him.

This was certainly not what the leaders of the council had planned. Hus's old teacher Stepan Páleč was present, and was tasked with convincing Hus to relent, and not to throw his life and ministry away. Páleč is said to have spent hours with Hus in his cell, weeping in frustration as Hus refused to accept the authority of other churchmen over him. So on July 6, 1415, Hus was taken out of the city of Konstanz and burnt at the stake. There are stories about this event, most notably the one in which the executioner said "Now we will cook the goose" as he applied the flame to the wood, to which Hus responded, "Yes but in a hundred years there will come an eagle you will not be able to catch," ostensibly prophesying the coming of Luther. This is a good story, but not a true one. He is better remembered for this, from his *Vyklad Víery*, "Therefore faithful Christian, seek the truth, listen to the truth, learn the truth, love the truth, speak the truth, adhere to truth, and defend truth to the death."

Was Hus guilty of these charges? Paul De Vooght has argued vigorously that Hus was innocent of all of them, and so was wrongfully burned for heresy. This is certainly the opinion of many who read or study Hus, and it is easy to conclude that Wyclif was already dead, and so was burned by proxy with Hus standing in for him. Thomas Fudge has recently argued that Hus was, in fact, guilty of heresy, because there are two parts to the crime: heterodoxy and contumely. While Hus may or may not have been guilty of any of the forty charges made against him, he was certainly contumacious in refusing to recognize the legitimacy of the ecclesiastical court in which he was tried. In claiming that Christ alone was his judge, he demonstrated his heresy according to canon law, and was duly punished according to that law. It is notable that on December 17, 1999, Pope John Paul II expressed sorrow for Hus's cruel death, leading some to expect his exoneration in months to come, which never happened. By the Vatican's understanding of the law, Hus remained guilty of heresy, despite the general opinion that he was not guilty of heterodoxy.

Hus's understanding of the church is at the centre of his theology. Following Augustine, it had long been agreed that the church is, in a real sense, the congregation of the Elect, those eternally foreknown for salvation. But given that human beings lack the wherewithal to read God's mind, Christians must turn to the institution organized by Christ as His body on earth, the church that began with the first disciples and has grown into the organization that it is today. Wyclif and Hus both raised the issue of those who function as ministers and officials in that organization who are manifestly breaking the laws Christ set forth in the gospels. Wyclif's argument was that anyone claiming the office of lordship, whether sacred or secular, must have been selected by God to do so and empowered with grace; those who used this position to live sinfully must no longer enjoy the favour of grace, and so occupy their offices wrongly. He is very close to Donatism here, the heresy in which sacraments are regarded as invalid when they are administered by morally impure ministers. That he also argues that preaching is more important to the Christian life than the sacraments only reinforces matters. But Wyclif expressly says that it is the business of civil lords to correct the abuses of errant clergy, and that they should employ bishops as moral enforcers. The result is that only grace-favoured lords are able to distinguish between true and false Christians through special revelation. Hus's argument was different, in that he followed Matěj by addressing his attention to hypocrisy as the chief symptom of clerical abuse of office. His preaching emphasized the gospel rules for right and wrong behaviour, thereby giving all his hearers the wherewithal to recognize sinful behaviour. Hus was not terribly clear about whether to use secular power, higher clerical authority, or the moral force of the clergy in general to correct the abuses, but he did encourage the laity to divest the clergy when their abuses were manifest. While he never actually said that one can tell who is elect and who is not, his zeal in encouraging immediate correction of clerical abuses by other clergy and the laity suggests that, at the least, those clergy who would resist correction must be likely to be damned. This democratization of reform is the "pernicious error" that horrified his contemporaries, and it has its roots in both Wyclif and Matěj.

At first, Jerome of Prague's membership among the prime movers of Hussitism is not obvious. His few remaining works are either abstract arguments about Wyclif's metaphysics, or they are letters sent to nobles and bishops. The one theological tract that remains, "The Shield of Faith," is a brief description of how to understand the relation of the three persons of the Trinity. Yet the theologians at Konstanz regarded Jerome as being as great a threat as Hus. The reason for this becomes evident only when we consider his career in the context of the reasons for which the Council at Konstanz had been convened. Jerome was a vigorous apostle of Wyclif, tirelessly championing his master's ideas against the theology of the *moderni* across Europe.

The *moderni* movement, inaugurated by William Ockham at the beginning of the fourteenth century, was based on distinguishing the logic of the Christian faith and Scripture from the logic of the Aristotelian natural sciences. Ockham and his followers reasoned that if God's power is so great as to permit biblical miracles, then God could conceivably have reason to cause us to perceive reality inaccurately, which is a step away from scepticism. Rather than attempt to create a system that skirts this problem, Ockham distinguished between the science with which we understand God and the faith and that with which we understand created reality. The two sciences are distinct, each relevant to its own reign of discourse. Twenty-first century readers may be surprised to learn that the scientific revolution of the sixteenth century has its roots in fourteenth-century theology, but Ockham's thought prepared the way for what we understand as modern scientific reasoning.

An important part of the *moderni* movement was the application of ancient political theory to church government. By the mid-fourteenth century, the hierarchical structure of the imperial papacy was beginning to show signs of strain, not least in the acrimonious contest between two competing popes. Ockham had applied the reasoning of Aristotle's *Politics* to church government, suggesting that a division of power and authority across sacred and secular offices would better serve the church's administrative needs. Their followers, many of them experts in canon law and its Roman jurisprudential foundations, formed the conciliarist movement. For them, Scriptural reasoning and natural reasoning could together develop a new governmental structure for the church, more republican than monarchic. As Thomas Fudge has recently observed, Jerome of Prague's advocacy of Wyclif posed a greater threat to conciliarism than either of the two popes. Jerome, following Wyclif and his predecessors, absolutely rejected the division of theological and natural reasoning. Wyclif had argued that the Bible contains all truth, and the logic behind interpreting it is the same that orders all creation. Rather than synthesizing the logic of faith and reason, as Thomas Aquinas and Duns Scotus had done, Wyclif's vision was of Scripture as the sole arbiter of all truth. Any apparent truth that either denied Scripture or cast a part of it into doubt was simply illusion. As Jerome travelled across Europe, he relished defending Wyclif's bibliolatrous rejection of the *moderni,* drawing attention to the many compromises he described animating their theology.

Jerome was never ordained but became known throughout Bohemia as an energetic and inventive speaker, as well as a dynamic physical presence. He began his career as Wyclif's apostle in Paris in 1403, defending his master's metaphyics and angering Jean Gerson, the chancellor of the university. Next, he did the same at the University of Köln in 1406, and again in Heidelberg later that year. 1407 found Jerome back in Prague, where he continued to proselytize for Wyclif. He was pivotal in a famous quodlibetal disputation in 1409 on Wycliffism, when Archbishop Zbyněk condemned it. He travelled throughout central Europe, landing in a prison in Vienna for heresy in 1410. After he escaped from prison, his reputation as a freelance Wyclif troublemaker grew until he was arrested and tried for heresy at Konstanz in April 1415. After Hus was burned that July, Jerome recanted, which the council regarded as a victory, given its failure with Hus. Gerson, Jerome's Inspector Javert, was publicly sceptical of Jerome's sincerity, and convinced the council to call him back for another trial in April 1416. This time, Jerome was imprisoned and tortured, and he decided that he had dissembled long enough. In a dramatic *volte face,* Jerome revoked his recantation, rebuking the assembled bishops and cardinals for murdering Hus on trumped up charges. He was condemned, of course, and shortly before his execution on May 30, he explained that his recantation was the result of his own fear. "I have failed like a lunatic, and I regret it very much, especially when I recanted the teaching of Jan Hus and John Wyclif, and when I agreed with the condemnation of Hus, because I believe him to be a just and holy man, and I have done this most wrongly." His trial and execution particularly impressed the Humanist scholar Poggio Bracciolini, whose account of it is particularly harrowing.

The deaths of Hus and Jerome of Prague left the reform movement in need of leadership, both theological and political. For a period of ten years, two figures dominated the movement: Jakoubek of Stříbro the theologian, and Jan Žižka the soldier. Žižka, who died in 1424, will figure in the next chapter, while this one introduces Jakoubek, whom Paul De Vooght rightfully described as *premier théologien du hussitisme*. Jakoubek remains almost unknown outside of Czech scholarship, despite having been the architect of Hussitism. Jakoubek of Stříbro, or Jacobellus of Mies, was born near Plzeň (Pilsen) in Bohemia in 1372, completed his baccalaureate studies at Charles University in 1393, and graduated as master of arts four years later. He was one of the Czech scholars fascinated by Wycliffism, and became active in Hus's circle by 1409, when he was a priest at St. Michael's in Prague. By 1414, he concluded that the laity were being wrongfully denied access to the chalice at Eucharist, and his arguments were quickly adopted by others in the Hus circle after Hus had departed for Konstanz. After Hus's death, Jakoubek joined three other Czech priests, Jan Želivský, Jan Přibram, and Procop of Plzeň, in organizing and preaching reform. Of these, he was the most prolific and respected theological mind, which led to the active part he played in formulating the Articles of Prague in 1421. He remained at the centre of the movement until his death in 1429. While he lived, he was the theological analogue to the military Žižka, mediating the increasingly contentious relation between conservative Prague and radical Tábor through a theological *via media* held together by the force of his personality. Just as the Hussite political balance never really recovered after Žižka's death, neither did the movement's theological unity survive Jakoubek's.

Relatively few of Jakoubek's works are easily available to the modern scholar. Seventy-seven works remain, including sermons, treatises, public correspondence, and brief *quaestiones*. Of these, slightly more than half have been edited, most in late-nineteenth and early-twentieth-century Czech editions. The most important non-Czech study of Jakoubek remains Paul De Vooght's 1972 French monograph, which also contains three previously un-edited works. Recently, Pavel Soukup has published a Czech-language study of Jakoubek's sermons that has breathed new life into Jakoubek studies. Both emphasize Jakoubek's apocalyptic vision as central to his understanding of reform. Jakoubek wrote a treatise on antichrist in 1412 warning that malign, demonic forces were at work in the church in the guise of apostolic authority. The profligate displays of wealth, political authority, and worldly morality demonstrated by the princes of the church proclaim a direct denial of Christ's teaching and moral example. It is rare indeed, Jakoubek observes, to find a preacher willing to name this scourge accurately. Jan Milíč was one such brave preacher, fearlessly indicting the church hierarchy for its complicity in antichrist's works. In a sermon written after 1417, he follows this line of reasoning in lifting up Hus and Jerome as examples of similarly grace-inspired preachers. In 1905, Vlastimil Kybal, the modern editor of Matěj of Janov, noticed that Jakoubek had made liberal use of Matěj's lengthy treatise on antichrist, and it is clear that his comparison of Hus to Milíč in a later sermon was likewise inspired by Matěj.

Jakoubek's Eucharistic theology was the first important contribution Bohemians would make to the ongoing question of how to understand Christ's presence in the consecrated elements. The doctrine of transubstantiation, in which the properties of the bread and wine remain whilst the essential natures are transformed into the body and blood of Christ, had been declared the correct interpretation of the sacrament at Lateran IV in 1215, and theologians had been working thereafter to explain it. Many theologians exerted their imaginative abilities to make the doctrine fit with Aristotelian physics, and Wyclif had been the first to absolutely reject the doctrine in 1380, which played an important role in his heretication. Stanislaus of Znojmo had written a treatise in 1405 in support of Wyclif, who had advocated remanentism, which as the name suggests, holds that the bread and wine remain substantially the same. Still, Wyclif advocated a real presence of Christ in the consecrated elements, even if that presence does not involve change in their essences or properties; but he was not quite clear what the "spiritual" reality of Christ's presence involved, which led his opponents to interpret Wyclif and his followers as having advocated no real change occurring in consecration. Jakoubek wrote several shorter pieces and three major treatises, one in 1415, a list of the errors of the Pickharts in 1421, and a final treatise in 1428, arguing that the real presence of Christ involved Christ's substantial and essential presence in the elements without Christ's actual substance or essence being physically present. Rather than claim a substantial change, Jakoubek argued for the acquisition of a new perfection with the introduction of Christ's essence. If there is no physical change, though, what occurs when the elements are consecrated? Jakoubek responded that the elements attain a mystic union with Christ whereby the individual consuming them is brought closer to Christ, shifting the explanation from Aristotelian physics to a more Platonic account of the effects of receiving the sacrament.

How does this distinguish Jakoubek from Wyclif? De Vooght points out that Jakoubek uses different Scriptural and patristic authorities to make his case, and a different rhetorical style, absent the alternation between complex metaphysics and vituperative criticism that Wyclif had adopted. The effect is the same, though; both were remanentists, advocates of real presence without specific Aristotelian physical explanations. The difference between the two arises from their consideration of the place of the sacrament in the Christian life. For Wyclif, the Eucharist had been turned into a means whereby the clergy could gain access to greater authority without actually having to embody Christ's moral example, while for Jakoubek, the sacrament was so important as to require it to be administered as often as possible with lay access to both bread and wine. For centuries, receiving the sacrament meant receiving consecrated bread, leaving the clergy to share the chalice amongst themselves. The doctrine of concomitance holds that each element contains all the benefits of the sacrament; indeed, in some cases the practice had developed that the laity could receive the benefits simply by casting their eyes on the consecrated host. Jakoubek seems to have developed the idea that the laity must receive both elements around the time Hus went to Konstanz, likely the result of conversations with Nicholas of

Dresden. Christ's command in John 5:53–56, Matthew 26:22–25, and Luke 22:19–20 is not equivocal: both body and blood are to be consumed, and Jakoubek notes that Cyprian, Gelasius II, and Albert the Great had affirmed this. The Utraquist idea caught on quickly in Prague, garnering the support of the conservative university masters and nobles, so that by 1421 it was included among the Four Articles. By the time of the victory at Vitkov hill in June 1420, the emblem of the chalice represented the movement as a whole.

Jakoubek's first debt is to Matěj, who imagined a church revived and strengthened by daily Eucharist, thereby able to ward off the depredations of antichrist. The doctrine of utraquism followed logically on Matěj's reasoning, given the commands in Scripture. As a theologian of the Eucharist, his debt to Wyclif is in perceiving the utility of shifting the discussion away from Aristotelian metaphysics and towards emphasis on the effects of the sacrament in the believer. His true debt to Wyclif lies in his ecclesiology. Both called for a priesthood relieved of property ownership and secular authority, and for a vision of church governance based more in Scripture than human political thought. Unlike Hus, Jakoubek stopped short of saying that the church is nothing other than the congregation of the Elect, perhaps because of the determinism that arose from it. Instead, he preferred Matěj's approach, describing the church in terms of communion. There are three ways of understanding the term: as the mystical body of Christ on earth, as the sacrament of Eucharist, and as the congregation of believers. The latter is a mixed body of the Elect and the damned for Jakoubek, a communion now imperilled by Satan and his tool, antichrist.

Iconoclasm was another important part of the Hussite theology, and Jakoubek was instrumental in encouraging a general rejection of paintings, statues, and other images of holy figures. Both Wyclif and Matěj had been likewise sceptical of anything suggesting veneration of images and statues, although Matěj had later been compelled to retract his criticisms. Jakoubek raged that so many signs and symbols invented by people have been brought into worship that

Christians do not know which are from God and which we have invented. The result is that when someone criticizes a human invention, it is as if he has transgressed against God! Art as such was not the problem, though; Jakoubek's objections were to the uses to which art was being put, drawing the thoughts of the faithful away from the body of Christ as the foundation of faith and towards the aesthetics of its presentation in the church. The same held true for venerating holy objects and relics, which elevated created bodies far above their true worth. This was little more than idolatry. The body of Christ is a mystic communion, and not built up by the accumulation of its members' limbs.

As do Wyclif and Hus, Jakoubek rejects the concept of the church as the juridical, hierarchical structure based in Rome in favour of a pure, universal church. He was as dubious regarding the validity of councils as he was about papal claims to authority. He did not produce a treatise on the church, though, as Wyclif and Hus had done, but his *Tractatus responsivus*, mistakenly edited and published by S. H. Thomson as the work of Hus, provides an excellent source for understanding Jakoubek's vision of the church. The treatise addresses the papacy, clerical sin and property ownership, indulgences, and excommunication. Papal claims to fulness of power are questionable, he argues, because Christ granted powers to those who follow Him with faith, not living in mortal sin. Simoniacs, hypocrites, and the wicked do not have these powers. People may decide that someone is Christ's vicar, but people are fallible and their mistakes inevitably come to light. While the sacramental power given with ordination surpasses human understanding, those who are ordained yet remain manifestly sinful do the church no good. This is not to say that sinful priests lose the power of administering the sacraments, because God provides gifts without regard to the moral purity of His ministers. But a priest who lives an evil life cannot provide the example Christians need, and one of the surest means of inclining a priest to an evil life is property ownership. Worse is the secular authority that inevitably follows upon ownership, and the present practice of selling indulgences, Jakoubek continues, is obviously an abuse of clerical power arising from a thirst for ownership and power. Indulgences may once have had a place in the church, but now they are so obviously a means by which the clergy abuse their authority by commodifying penance.

Excommunication is the final abuse Jakoubek attacks in the treatise, which topic leads inevitably back to his three-fold definition of communion. From which communion does the practice of excommunication exclude someone? It seems that it must be the third, the community of believers we understand to be the church. But if one is already a member of Christ's mystical body, they cannot rightly be denied Eucharist, and so cannot be removed from the community of believers. Hence, the pope's claim to have the power to excommunicate anyone is ill-founded. This criticism fits neatly with the doctrine that the church is the invisible body of the Elect, which Wyclif and Hus supported. In fact, the whole of the *Tractatus responsivus* is filled with quotations from Wyclif's works, and articulates Hus's positions from *De ecclesia*, which was what led Thomson to believe the work to be Hus's. But the determinism that defines the church of Hus and Wyclif is completely absent from the *Tractatus*. This matters because the question of determinism and predestination was one of the divisive issues for the generation of Hussite theologians who followed Jakoubek. The Prague Hussites Jan Příbram and Jan Rokycana both rejected the determinist model of the church that Hus and Wyclif had presented, while Peter Payne and Biskupec, the leading figures of the Táborite movement, embraced it. Jakoubek's accomplishment was to construct a theological *via media* that satisfied both Prague and Tábor, a balance that would not survive him.

Hus, Jerome of Prague, and Jakoubek represent the theologians who embodied a more conservative Hussite position. The radical position, ultimately championed by Tábor, was first articulated by a group of Germans from Dresden who gravitated towards Prague around 1411, when they heard of Hus and his followers. The most important of these was Nicholas of Dresden, who would work closely with Jakoubek as the

Hussite theology took a coherent form. The Dresden school had already redefined the church the way Hus and Wyclif did, but their approach relied on juxtaposing opposite ideals in theory and practice: the true communion of the elect versus the false church of antichrist. Nicholas argued that the first iteration of the church, the apostolic community, was the opposite of the corporate behemoth now calling itself the Roman church. The evidence was everywhere: Christ rode into Jerusalem on an ass, the Pope processes on a stallion; the membership of the apostolic church was a community of equals, while the present institution is defined by hierarchic complexity; the apostolic church shared everything in common, while the present institution owns one third of Europe.

For Nicholas of Dresden the perversion of Eucharist typifies the present institution's corruption. While the early faithful shared bread and cup in harmonious equality, the present arrangement allots the laity some of the bread and no wine. This is symptomatic of the grave division that has afflicted the church over the centuries. Nicholas seems to have come to this conclusion at roughly the same time as Jakoubek did, who is said to have learned of the Orthodox practice of sharing a common cup from Jerome of Prague. It seems likely that, given the close relations between Nicholas and Jakoubek in 1414, the two should be ranked as co-originators of Bohemian utraquism. Nicholas continued his radical criticism of the church after Hus died, gradually moving towards a Waldensian social vision and away from the church reform Jakoubek supported. Nicholas argued that all Christians should preach, all priests are equal, singing and praying should occur in the soul, not the church, oaths should not be sworn, and all murder is forbidden. Purgatory is a myth, and confession does not need an intermediary priest to be valid. By 1416, Nicholas recognized that his vision of reform exceeded the Bohemian vision, and he left Prague and the historical record.

## Prague versus Tábor: Přibram, Rokycana, Biskupec, Payne

The next phase in the development of Hussite thought began after Jakoubek died in 1429, when the division between Tábor and Prague became irreparable. Four figures dominated Hussite theology in the latter period of the Hussite war: two represented the conservative Prague community of reform-minded university masters and lesser nobility (Jan Přibram, d. 1448, and Jan Rokycana, d. 1471), one represented the radical Táborite cause (Nicholas "Biskupec" of Pehlřimov, d. 1459), and one made a name for himself representing the Hussites in courts and councils across Europe (Peter Payne, also known as Peter "Engliš," d. 1455). The internal conflict between Prague and Tábor eventually did what neither emperor nor pope could. It drove the Prague Hussites to compromise with the emperor and defeat Tábor at Lipany in 1435, thereby ending the Hussite war.

Jan Rokycana was born in 1397, son of a blacksmith, near Plzeň in Bohemia. He studied at Prague University, receiving his baccalaureate degree in 1415. During those years, he attended Bethlehem chapel, where he was captivated by Hus, and adopted as a student by Jakoubek. After Želivsky's attempted coup in 1422, Rokycana fled Prague, and two years later he was engaged in mediating between the Prague Hussites and Žižka. He was ordained in 1427 and made rector of the Church of the Virgin near Tyn church in the Old Town of Prague. He rose quickly among the Hussites there and was chosen leader of the Utraquist pastors in 1430, when he became Master of Arts. He was a leader among the deputies of the Hussite delegation in 1433 to the Council of Basel. While the Council of Basel resolved little, Rokycana returned to Prague highly regarded by his fellow Hussites. He was named rector of Prague University in 1435, and was elected archbishop of Prague that same year. Pope Martin V refused to recognize the appointment, but Rokycana functioned as archbishop for the Utraquist church thereafter. He lived outside of Prague for the next thirteen years, and allied himself with Jiří Poděbradý, who became king of Bohemia in 1458. Rokycana returned to Prague in 1448, where he took up residence at the Tyn church, and began to be involved with the nascent *Unitas fratrum* movement at Emmaus cloister. Rokycana dominated the Hussite movement during the years after Lipany, serving Jiři as mediator between church and state, and in diplomacy with neighbouring Catholic countries. In 1465 he engaged in a heated controversy on the Utraquist side with the Catholic church, an unsuccessful attempt by Jiři to achieve better relations with Rome. Rokycana died in 1471 and was buried in the Tun church, although he was later exhumed and buried elsewhere with the return of Catholicism in the seventeenth century. He was not a formal theologian, and while Bartoš lists close to fifty works in his catalogue, most are either sermons or diplomatic or ecclesiastical–political writings, few of which have been edited.

Jan Přibram represented the conservative wing in the Hussite party. He was born in Přibram in central Bohemia in 1387 and studied at Prague University with Biskupec and Jakoubek. In the years following Hus's death, Přibram was close to Jakoubek, and was involved with him in the formulation of the four articles of Prague in 1421. The rise of Tábor led to a divide between Jakoubek and Přibram, and the latter was aggressive and indefatigable in opposing the Pickharts, Tábor, and Želivsky in the coming years. Přibram supported the Eucharistic theory of transubstantiation, which led him to confront Jakoubek and, eventually, Peter Payne. Přibram was probably Payne's most determined opponent among the Hussites, and did not hesitate to use any criticism available in his arguments, including casting aspersions on his nationality. Přibram's conservative position appealed to Sigismund Korybut, the Polish–Lithuanian duke the Hussites had asked to reign as Bohemian king in 1421, but when Korybut was compelled to leave Prague in 1423, Přibram became less powerful in the Hussite movement, and he left Prague in 1427 for nine years. He regained his position as the division between Prague and Tábor widened, and in 1437 was selected to join the Hussite legislation to Basel, where he defended both the Utraquist position and the more controversial Hussite willingness to allow children to take Eucharist. He continued to engage in polemical attacks on Tábor and adherents of Wycliffism, and when the possibility to participate in the legation that agreed on a Hussite–Catholic alliance to defeat Tábor, he was glad to play a role in negotiations. He remained active in Prague thereafter, serving as deacon of the university in 1438, and arguing in 1441 for a merger of the Hussite church with Rome, based primarily on his continuing antipathy for Wycliffism. Rokycana opposed this, and on his death in 1448 Příbram was remembered as a stalwart advocate of a conservative version of Hussitism that permitted utraquism but rejected the radicalism of Tábor.

The Tábor community was founded in South Bohemia in 1420 as a base from which Jan Žižka, the Hussite military general, could organize and deploy his forces against his enemies. From its beginning, the community was organized on the understanding that the great trial of the Apocalypse was at hand. Tábor represented the beginning of a new social order that would emerge as Christ overcame antichrist and established His new earthly kingdom. The radical preacher Koranda inspired the Táborites to adopt a communitarian social structure organized around daily sermons directing life according to a Scripturally-based Law of God. The difference between the apostolic church and Tábor, though, lie in promulgation of the Word. Tábor was dedicated to spreading the true Christianity by armed force. The depredations of antichrist had turned Christendom so far from its ideal form that the only resort was ongoing warfare against the forces of evil. This meant travelling in armed bands from town to village, overcoming any resistance the locals might offer, and forcibly restructuring them to fit the strict moral and social codes of Tábor. Diocesan priests were usually executed, and all were compelled to put their belongings into a common pile in the town square as contribution to the communitarian ideal. Those hiding private possessions were severely punished. Táborites ranged across Bohemia, into Bavaria and Moravia, and in the last years of the Hussite wars, into Poland and the Baltic states. As we will see,

Tábor would serve the Soviets very well in their propagandistic rearrangement of Czech history.

Nicholas, born in Pehlřimov, south-east of Prague and west of Tábor, studied in Prague and was drawn into the circle of Hus's admirers. After Hus died, Nicholas became a priest in Kondrace, another small town in southern Bohemia, but by 1420, he returned to Prague. He gravitated naturally to the newly founded Táborite cause and became a spokesman for the clergy at the centre of the Táborite brotherhood. Tábor's attitude towards the Four Articles was that they were a good beginning, but still fairly tepid. Táborite priests dispensed with vestments, ornaments, and excessive ritual, to allow Christians to focus on Christ rather than earthly things. Nicholas, as intellectual force behind the brotherhood, was elected unofficial "bishop" in December 1420. As Tábor's "little bishop" (*biskupec*), he represented Tábor at negotiations with Prague, which were almost never smooth; he regularly angered Jan Přibram and tested Jakoubek's patience.

The differences between Prague and Tábor were stark not only theologically, but politically. Both Jakoubek and Biskupec agreed that antichrist was ushering in the End Times, but their responses were very different. Rather than reforming the church through daily Eucharist at all levels, Biskupec demanded an absolute reformation of all levels of Christian society. Since property ownership is based in sin, secular lords have no business interfering in Christian life, so Biskupec rejected the Wycliffite ideal of a top-down reformation led by a righteous civil lord. Instead, he envisioned a priest-directed church-state, without class, ownership, or social division. As mentioned, he was not reticent in instructing his fellow Christians in this. Little wonder that the Prague Hussites recoiled in horror from Tábor. The clash of the two ideologies foreshadowed the ongoing conflict about the place of religion in society that defined the centuries to come. Thomas Fudge has reflected that Tábor became less a particular location in southern Bohemia than an idea the Táborites carried around with them, and an ideology that led eventually to compromise between Prague and Rome.

Biskupec may have angered Přibram and been a trial to Jakoubek and Rokycana, but he intrigued Peter Payne. Payne, an Oxford proponent of Wyclif years after Wycliffism had been condemned there, journeyed to Prague in late 1414. Known as "English Peter," he became friendly with Jakoubek who admired his intellectual talents and began to rely on him to represent the reform movement in Germany and Poland. A skilled philosopher, he was able to maintain a theological balance between Prague and Tábor, and by 1429 he had gained sufficient reputation to represent the Hussites to Emperor Sigismund in Bratislava. Later that year, after Jakoubek's death, Payne clashed with Přibram, who despised Wycliffism, in a two-day disputation in Prague. This earned him Tábor's respect, who engaged him to represent them to the king of Poland in 1431. The failure of the fourth crusade against the Hussites later that year led to an invitation to leading Hussite theologians to present their case at the ecumenical council in Basel. By this time, Jan Rokycana had risen to prominence among the Prague Hussites, and he appointed Payne to the delegation. After three months of "frank discussions," the Hussites left Basel unharmed in April 1433.

Payne remained in a mediating position between Rokycana and Biskupec for the next year, until the battle of Lipany on May 30, 1434. Still a confirmed Wycliffite, Payne struggled to maintain his position in a Bohemia now governed by Sigismund and the Prague Hussites. The Hussites may have achieved a final victory at Lipany, but Wycliffism was defeated there, and Payne spent time imprisoned by a Catholic noble from 1438 to 1440. He continued to engage in formal disputations with Přibram, who by this time must have simply enjoyed sparring with his English adversary. It is likely that Payne lived to 1456, spending his final years as an advisor to the now Archbishop Jan Rokycana. He was not a prolific writer, but the few works of his there are show a sharp intellect. He was not above using his wits to confuse his opponents; his defence of the Hussite position regarding clerical ownership at Basel included extensive citations from Wyclif that he claimed to be from Archbishop FitzRalph. While Wyclif had made liberal use of FitzRalph in his work, of which his auditors were certainly aware, the sections Payne cites were not the words of the doctrinally exemplary Irish archbishop, but those of the Oxford heresiarch.

Biskupec, too, survived the fall of Tábor, but unlike Payne, he spent the last years of his life imprisoned by the Hussite king, Jiří Poděbradý. Biskupec did not sit idle, though, compiling a commentary on the gospels and another on John's Apocalypse. These two vast works, today still unedited, provide an extensive introduction to the Táborite hermeneutic of Scripture. The *Harmonium Evangelicarum*, for example, arranged according to the traditional Eusebian canon groupings, presents Biskupec's favourite commentators for the gospels, including the pseudo-Chrysostom's *Opus Imperfectum*, Origen, Gregory the Great, and, more recently, Nicholas of Lyra and Wyclif. Earlier, Biskupec had written two narratives of the ideological disputes Tábor had with Prague. In the *Chronicon Táboritarum*, Biakupec and Johannis de Lukavecz record the details of each doctrinal disputation and formal confrontation, from Tábor's beginnings in 1424 to well past Lipany in three volumes. The *Confessio Táboritarum* is divided into a careful doctrinal exposition of Tábor's theology, and a response to Jan Rokycana's list of seven Táborite errors. Together, the *Chronicon* and the *Confessio* present the reasoning behind the radical Táborite position.

Jan Rokycana articulated seven errors that defined Tábor's spirituality in 1431, which Biskupec refuted point by point, after complaining that Rokycana and the Prague theologians rely too heavily on sophistry and logical trickery foreign to God's law. Why should Christians rely on the efficacy of sacraments like extreme unction and confirmation that have no biblical precedent? Why should they be expected to pray for the dead and hope that one's good works will expiate their sins? Indeed, what good comes from praying to saints, rather than to Christ or God? The church has taught that fasting is good for the soul, which may be so, but its legalistic account of what does or does not count as fasting makes the practice pharisaical. Rokycana then criticized the Táborite readiness to wage war against God's enemies, but does he not recall that it was the bishops at Konstanz that began the war by murdering Hus? And why shouldn't Tábor seek to overthrow civil lords that disobey God's law? Does their invented title shield them from Christ's sure judgment? Finally, Rokycana castigates Tábor for abandoning the standard liturgical practices in the Mass, which even Wyclif upheld as important, but Biskupec retorts that Rokycana is reading too much into Wyclif's words: communion, not liturgy, is the point of the Mass.

Of these seven faults, four have to do with Christian practice of daily worship, two concern Tábor's political practices, and one addresses sacramental liturgy. It is difficult today to see how these seven issues would be enough to divide two groups who have so much else—language, culture, a common enemy—to unite them. But underlying these differences were two fundamentally opposed Christian ideologies. Prague Hussites did not imagine themselves to be creating a new social order, preferring instead to steer the established secular and ecclesiastical structures back to the stability they had enjoyed in earlier times. Tábor envisioned a new world, in which all human beings lived in a perfected earthly kingdom defined only by God's law as described in Scripture. One envisioned a return to the ancient exemplar of the apostolic church, while the other was convinced that history itself was near an end, and that a new *eschaton* was at hand.

## Petr Chelčický

The Utraquist position would remain viable in Bohemia until the Thirty Years' War (1618-1648), even if Tábor had declined after Lipany. But the version of Hussitism that would, and does, endure, began with a remarkable thinker from Chelčicé in South Bohemia who was not a part of either Tábor or Prague. Petr Chelčický has been a slightly mysterious figure: he never went to university, was never ordained, and appears only to have left South Bohemia once, early in his career, to visit Prague. Bartoš has argued that Petr is likely to have been a member of the lower nobility from an estate near Chelčicé, perhaps the same as Petr Záhoriky from nearby Záhorčí, about whom little is known. Whatever his surname, Petr rejected scholastic theology, arguments from the authority of the church or the Fathers, and the theology of the preaching orders in favour of a *sola scriptura* approach to describing the Christian life. This is not to say that he had not read widely in theology. Petr seems to have been profoundly moved by Waldensians, who were concentrated in the area of Záhorči and Chelčicé, as well as by advocates of Bohemian reform such as Štitný, Hus, and later Jakoubek. He also demonstrates familiarity with Wyclif and kept abreast of the controversies at Basel.

Petr wrote extensively, in Czech, on the Christian life, and especially on the Scriptural description of the power of divine law in relation to human law. It was in discussing the applicability of the law that Petr was most original. In most medieval thought on the nature of justice and the law, it was necessary to give serious thought to Justinian and to Aristotelian political and ethical thought. Petr had none of that, arguing forcefully that all human law and the justice it embodies is grounded in compulsion through the threat of violence. Even the most benevolent and devout king is constrained to rely on the threat of physical punishment to ensure peace in his kingdom. Paul had counselled his congregations to obey secular authorities, but this did not mean that he regarded them as just. It was only to preserve the faith, to be inconspicuous in the face of pagan rule, but it did not mean tacit acceptance of its assumptions. When the church received the (subsequently shown to be false) "Donation of Constantine," purportedly giving the church authority over the Western Roman empire, it handed itself over to active cooperation in this abhorrent tradition of oppressive compulsion. A true Christian, Petr concluded, must not presume to take the law into his own hands, nor ought he permit his soul to be endangered by breaking divine commands at a king's word. Petr was a real anomaly in medieval thought: he understood Jesus to have taught anarchism and radical pacifism, even though both terms had yet to be invented when he wrote.

Petr was widely respected for his insight and his grasp of conveying the gospel message in the Czech language. Indeed, there was a strong element of Milíč in his teachings. He corresponded with Biskupec and Rokycana, sternly reprimanding them for using warfare and violence as a means to their end. While they appear not to have listened too closely to his advice, he was regarded very highly in both Tábor and Prague. After the Battle of Lipany, Petr began to attract followers from Tábor, Oreb, and from remaining Waldensian groups. When he died in 1458, a group of his followers under the leadership of Rokycana's nephew Řehoř (Gregory) carried on, as we will see in the next chapter. His works are not easy to find in translation. His longest work, *The Net of Faith*, has been partially translated by Amadeo Molnar, and is online, as is *On Spiritual Struggle*. Howard Kaminsky has translated *On the Three Peoples*, his most arresting criticism of the feudal structure, but most of his works remain available only in Czech. It is difficult to imagine Catholic authorities turning a blind eye to Petr's radical writings had he written in Latin, but it is possible that his use of the vernacular rendered him comparatively harmless.

Chapter 2

# Hussite History

This chapter will briefly survey the main events of the Hussite movement in the fifteenth century. This, in itself, is historiographically questionable, because although the fighting largely ended in 1435 at Lipany, the Hussite phenomenon continued to evolve into the Modern period. Complicating matters is the absence of historical narratives in English. The two most reputable accounts, those of Howard Kaminsky and Frederick Heymann, end with the death of Žižka in 1425. So, too, does the *Chronicle* of Laurence of Březova, the only account of the movement written by a Bohemian. There are much fuller accounts in Czech, of course, and František Šmahel's three-volume study was translated into German in 2002, but for Anglophones, the only complete overview remains Jiři Kejř's *The Hussite Revolution*, which was published in Prague in 1988, and is not readily available.

The Hussite movement had its origins in the reign of the emperor Charles IV, who dominated mid-fourteenth-century Europe. Bohemia was situated in the heart of the Holy Roman Empire, which stretched from the Low Countries to Gdańsk, and from the Piedmont to the Adriatic, encompassing what is today Austria, Germany, Switzerland, Croatia, Slovenia, the Netherlands, and the Czech-speaking lands of Bohemia, Moravia, and Silesia. Charles was the son of John the Blind of Luxembourg and Elizabeth of Bohemia, heiress of the Přemyslid dynasty that had once ruled the Czech lands. Though he was named Václav at birth, he took the name Charles to honour the French

Charles IV, his uncle, with whom he lived in his youth. He ruled the lands of the Bohemian crown in the 1340s, but until he was elected Holy Roman Emperor in 1355, he was regarded as an insignificant figure in European politics. Charles had prepared a strong political base for himself in Bohemia, and established Prague as a city to rival Vienna with a rigorous expansion program. He built churches, the eponymous bridge spanning the Vltava (Moldau), and a magnificent stronghold just south of the city, Karlstejn, which remains one of Europe's famous castles. Most significantly for this narrative, he founded a university in Prague in 1348 which he intended to put his city on an intellectual par with Paris. His "Golden Bull" of 1356 provided the basis for the secure regulation of the selection of future emperors for the next four centuries.

Charles had arranged for his two sons, Václav and Sigismund, to reign as Bohemian king and Holy Roman emperor respectively. Bohemia had become the centre of the Empire in the sense that merchants, intellectuals, artists, and churchmen were drawn there from across Europe, and the kingdom prospered. European stability faltered, though, after the Black Death of 1349 provided a blow to the agricultural and market systems, and the papal schism that developed towards the end of the century tore Europe into two opposing factions. A group of prominent theologians and ecclesiastics proposed establishing an ecumenical council to resolve the deadlock and restore some order to Latin Christianity. The reasoning behind this was classically Aristotelian. The church, analogous to the *polis*, was divided, resulting in widespread injustice and disorder. Reasoning that the papal monarchy had decayed into a tyranny, the theologians reasoned that the time had come for institution of a conciliar system of church government, patterned on the classical republican division of powers that had defined Rome. The opposing popes, of course, had no real interest in submitting to the judgment of a body of their juniors, but secular authorities like Emperor Sigismund supported the conciliarist idea.

In the meantime, Bohemia, the *quondam* home of the beloved Charles, was in an uproar with the sudden eruption of angry cries for reform from Prague. As described in the first chapter, call for church reform had begun there as Charles was expanding the city, and by the convocation of the council at Konstanz in 1413, the Hussite movement had become impossible to ignore. The conciliarist model was put to the test: the church was threatened with the spread of the Wycliffite/Hussite heresy in the heart of Europe, and the church leaders assembled in Konstanz needed to demonstrate that their republican model could contain the heresy. In inviting Hus to explain himself to the council, the conciliarists were committing to either his reconciliation or his death. The former would have been a great victory for the conciliarist cause, while Hus's death did little to help it.

Hus's death did not lead immediately to war, but it did exacerbate the division between Emperor Sigismund and the Czech nobles who had either supported Hus or, at least, had expected that the promise of safe conduct might mean something. Their dissent increased in late 1415 and so worried the council that they demanded that he pacify the nobles. Sigismund reminded the council that his brother Václav was king, but promised to do what he could. The council responded by issuing a list of twenty-four resolutions condemning the Hussite ideology in February 1418, reminding Václav that he had a duty to preserve the church in Bohemia. Not content to wait for Václav, the new pope Martin V commanded Sigismund to engage the heretics in Bohemia and established an inquisition to assist. By late April, this news reached Prague, and nobles and commoners alike were enraged.

The end of July can find Prague baking in summer heat, and on July 30, 1419, the city had reached boiling point. Jan Želivský, one of the radical Hussite cadre, preached an incendiary sermon at Our Lady of the Snows in Prague. Who, he asked, is worthy of the bread Christ gives to the faithful? "Those who commit deeds without any regard for the common good [...] who avoid work and flaunt themselves in the luxury for which others sweat are unworthy!" Everyone knew his targets: popes, bishops, and civil servants cynically disregarding the needs of common Christians. The congregation angrily swarmed out of the church and to the nearby New Town Hall, where they stormed past the guards and into the council chambers several stories above. They threw the city councillors out of the windows and onto the streets below, where the mob murdered them. This, the (first) defenestration of Prague signalled the beginning of open civil defiance of civil and church authorities. Václav IV died of a stroke two weeks later, and Lord Čenek of Vartenberk, Burgrave of Prague, notified Sigismund that the nobility would recognize him as his brother's successor to the Bohemian throne, provided that he support a version of the Hussite agenda. The emperor refused to respond.

By November, Hussite pilgrims moving through South Bohemia to Prague were attacked near Živhost and defeated by a noble in support of the rumoured crusade. News of this reached Prague, and the galvanized Hussites attacked and routed royal forces in Mala Strana. The uproar was not confined to Prague. At Kutná Hora, the silver-mining town east of Prague, the city council offered rewards for captured Hussites, and throughout that fall, over sixteen hundred people had been taken to the city. They were kept there in camps, and eventually all were hurled down the mine shafts to their deaths. Martin's papal condemnation of the Hussites in February 1418 was followed in March 1420 by a formal proclamation of a full-scale crusade against the Hussites, which Sigismund heartily endorsed. "I can scarcely wait for the day to come when I can drown every Wycliffite and Hussite."

By this point, Tábor had been established and was gaining a reputation for its fearless peasant army. Rather than recount the events of the many battles between the Hussites and their enemies, it will be useful to recount the general tactical approach that led to the Hussites' many victories. Jan Žižka of Trocno was a minor noble who had been a mercenary in the service of the king of Poland. Despite accidentally losing an eye while still young, he was a very successful soldier. By the time hostilities erupted in Bohemia, he was in his mid-sixties, but far from ready to retire. He had learned two important facts as a mercenary: horses will not kill themselves by charging into unmoving obstacles, and gunfire can kill a mounted knight more effectively than any other weapon. So Žižka worked with what he had available to him in developing Táborite tactics. He had little army, relatively few swords, and fewer trained swordsmen, and almost no cavalry. He did have sturdy peasants with great stamina and the usual array of agricultural tools to double as weapons: scythes, flails, and hammers. He also had hay wagons and draught horses, and skilled carpenters and smiths. So he put thick wooden sides with portholes on the wagons and taught the peasant drivers to manoeuvre a procession of wagons into a circle, with the horses tethered in the middle. Once this lager was formed, the peasants would set up small, portable cannon between the wagons. These were called "hufnitze," the origin of the word "howitzer." Protected behind pavises, or man-sized shields, some trained peasants would shoot "pistola," or pole-mounted handguns, just outside the lager. The majority would wait in the wagons with handguns, cross-bows, flails, and hand-made pole arms. Beneath the wagons, others would lie in wait with daggers and hatchets.

The standard battlefield attack in the later Middle Ages involved massed mounted knights thundering across the field to obliterate the opposing infantry. A strong and skilled knight in over one hundred pounds (fifty kilograms) of plate armour on a horse weighing up to a ton galloping with a lance into infantry was almost unstoppable; armoured lancers were the heavy cavalry of many modern armies into the nine-teenth century. So the knights would charge *en masse* with horns blasting and pennons flying into the lager, and were frustrated by their mounts' refusal to crash through the wag-ons. Hufnitze, handguns, and crossbows would pierce their armour, stunning if not immediately killing the knights. The peasants would hook the mounted knights with their make-shift pole arms or batter them with their flails. Most knights ended up on the ground, disoriented or in shock, weighted down with their heavy armour, and blinded by their heavy visors. At this point, the peasants under the wagons would emerge and carefully stab or hack at the joints of the armour, usually at the armpit, groin, or back of the knee. It does not take long to bleed to death from wounds in those locations.

Incredibly, this tactic would work time and again as the primary means by which Žižka would face the crusading German knights. That he tended to keep his army on the move made it difficult for the crusaders to field large infantry units against him, which meant that many of the Hussite battles involved relatively small units of mobile peasants with guns defeating much larger forces of mounted knights. In some cases, Žižka mounted his cannon on the wagons, and had his peasants push the wagons forward, stopping every so often to fire into the enemy. This tactic would not be used again until the Great War (1914–1918). Žižka was also innovative in his willingness to include women in his armies, a tactic that particularly infuriated the knights' chivalric sense of honour. While each Hussite battle differed in particular ways from the generic description here, each involved some version of combined gunfire and the lager. Žižka first employed it at Sudoměř, in Southern Bohemia. His forces were caught on the march by a larger body of Catholic cavalry between a swamp and a lake, and his improvised lager defence, coupled with a swift and merciless counterattack, set the pattern for future battles.

As spring 1420 turned into summer, soldiers from throughout Europe journeyed to Northern Bohemia, while the Hussites invested Prague and attempted a siege of the Vyšehrad castle there. The Bohemian nobility coalesced into a Hussite body, determined to oppose crusaders as an insult to the Czech people. "This is a severe dishonour, and a disgrace to the Czech language!" they angrily declared on April 20, and concluded their proclamation of mutual commitment: "Furthermore we wish for you to know that we stand for nothing other than these articles which follow. First, that the common people might receive the body and blood of the Lord in both kinds. Second, that the word of God might be properly and freely proclaimed. Third, that priests might live lives of exemplary conduct in the manner which our Lord Christ commanded along with the apostles and institutions of the holy fathers thereafter. Fourth, that the Czech language and king-dom be cleansed from all harmful rumours and slander for the common benefit of our kingdom and language of Bohemia." While this is not the final wording of the Four Articles, which would appear at the Diet of Časlav in 1421, its emphasis on the importance of the Czech language would figure importantly in the nation's history in centuries to come.

The crusading armies began massing outside of Prague that June, and the skirmishing began. The crusaders were enraged to find Bohemian women in Hussite raiding parties, and neither side bothered with keeping prisoners alive for long. Finally, Sigismund staged his main attack on the Hussites, who had occupied the long hill known as the Vitkov, the highest point of the city. Žižka ordered his soldiers to construct a log and stone fortress with two towers at the end of the hill with the steepest sides. At the other end of the hill, several thousand knights amassed on July 14, prepared to storm the improvised fortress. Following what he considered would be certain victory, Sigismund had other forces throughout the city prepared to sack the town in punishment for its support of the vanquished heretics. The crusaders charged across the long Vitkov hill and crashed into the bulwarks. What had seemed certain victory quickly devolved into chaos. Peasant men and women with flails knocked the knights from their mounts and down the steep incline of the hill, where other peasants waited among the rocks to finish the hapless warriors off. The narrow front of the fort meant that the defenders never really faced more crusaders than they were prepared to handle, as did the crusaders' foolish decision not to rely on archers to soften up the defences. Within an hour, Sigismund cancelled the attack and pulled back in disgust. Lacking the clear victory over Žižka he needed, he could not justify his crusaders sacking the second city of the Empire. Instead the crusaders left the city demoralized, and the hill became known as the Žižkov, as it remains today.

Hussitism attracted a number of non-conformist groups from across Europe, including advocates of an apocalyptically oriented chiliasm inspired by Joachim of Fiore, Waldensians, and the Brethren of the Free Spirit. A related group, known as the Pickharts (possibly a form of "Beghard") attached itself in large numbers to Tábor from 1418 to 1420. They believed, like gnostics, that they could attain an elevated state of sinlessness, rendering them saints when the millennial trials would begin. They were dismissive, if not derisory, regarding sacramental Christianity, and regarded themselves as free to respond to the Spirit in whatever way it moved them, which was usually erotically. While other "heretical" groups regarded themselves as realizing a purer form of Christianity, as the Pickhart numbers increased, it became clear that they believed that they had surpassed Christianity entirely. Táborite theology was still sufficiently fluid as to give the Pickharts reason to believe that their sect was welcome in the Bohemian reform movement, perhaps because so many Táborites shared their chiliastic anticipation of the apocalypse. While Tábor experimented in simplifying and "purifying" the Eucharistic liturgy, their Pickhart neighbours were shifting their devotional life away from sacramentalism altogether. By the end of 1420, the Pickharts had clearly defined themselves as a different sect, associated with Tábor and Prague mostly because of the protection they provided.

By winter 1421, Tábor had had enough of Pickhart debauchery, and expelled several hundred of them from the settlement. They moved to a village not far away and stepped up their innovations by introducing ritual nudism and an even more unbridled attitude towards sexuality. At this point, the name "Adamite" became synonymous for "Pickhart." Biskupec and other Táborite leaders sensed the grave danger their quondam allies posed as Tábor struggled to gain credibility with Prague, and Žižka began active raids on the Adamite village that April. Žižka took about seventy-five prisoners and burned them all for heresy. The Adamites fled further south, with Žižka in pursuit; finally, on October 21, 1421, Žižka defeated them in a fierce battle and massacred the survivors. Rumours of Adamites or Pickharts continued through the 1420s, but as a coherent sect, they had been obliterated.

The tension between Tábor's radicalism and Prague's moderate approach was particularly evident when the two sides met to find common ground on how to celebrate Eucharist. While the more conservative parties in Prague were open to Jakoubek's advocacy of the lay chalice, they reacted especially negatively to Táborite liturgical simplification. The two parties met for public disputations frequently in 1420 and 1421, with Biskupec generally debating Příbram as the Hussite forces won victory after victory. The leaders of both parties agreed that the time was right for a general meeting, including Catholics as well as Prague and Tábor Hussites, and set the day of June 3, 1421 for a diet at Čáslav. All agreed that discussing politics would be more important than arguing about religious differences, so two theologians were appointed to represent the two Hussite positions, Jan Příbram and Jan Želivský. Želivský, whose preaching had instigated the defenestration in 1419, had gathered a notable following in Prague, and managed to coordinate the appointments of several radical priests for important pulpits in the Old Town. In so doing, he had managed to press the radical agenda into ordinarily conservative territory in the Prague university section. Talk began about Želivský making a bid to unite Prague and Tábor into one radical Hussite bloc.

When the parties met at Čáslav, the Catholics failed to show. For a time, Jakoubek managed to balance the radical and conservative agendas, but his patience with Želivský soon frayed. As he began to perceive the radical priest as at the centre of an attempted coup to gain control of the whole movement, he became very alarmed. Kaminsky probably accurately speculates that Jakoubek had begun to associate Želivský as an agent of antichrist. The coming weeks found Prague bitterly divided between Želivský and the Táborites on the one hand, and the conservative faction led by Jakoubek and Příbram on the other. Želivský cannily used his political base to his advantage in political skirmishes, but fell into a trap when he met with a group of city magistrates on March 9, 1422. After a short discussion, he and his party were arrested, frogmarched out to Old Town Square, and beheaded. Public relations between Želivský's faction and the conservatives remained bad for several months. Today the visitor to Old Town Square can find a plaque dedicated to Želivský on the clock tower, a lone monument to the brief period in which Tábor almost controlled the whole Hussite revolution.

Sigismund had not been deterred by the defeat on the Vitkov hill in Prague in July 1420. Nor did he learn to respect his adversaries who had surrounded the Vyšehrad castle in Prague that fall. While the emperor fought Hussites west of Prague, the Hussites compelled the starving Vyšehrad garrison to surrender by November 1. Sigismund arrived to relieve the siege on October 20, and was humiliatingly defeated. The Hussite victory at the Vyšehrad led to publication of a manifesto defining the essentially Czech nature of the movement. It claimed Sigismund had put his Czech soldiers in the front lines, and had seduced them to abandon the true faith, murdering them "in order to weaken our Czech language."[1]

The war spread across Bohemia, with battles in Přebenice, Prachatice, Strážnice, Chotěboř, and Chomutov bitterly dividing the people. Sigismund decided to try again in May 1421, and encouraged his Silesian nobles to invade north-eastern Bohemia while the Časlav diet met. Želivský was defeated while fighting them that August, and the crusaders made their genocidal intent clear in a letter dated September 1, 1421. "Everyone must be killed in the land of Bohemia, with the exception of children who are not yet at the age of reason. No women are to be taken [...]."[2] They laid siege to the Hussite town of Žatec that summer, but when they learned that Žižka and his army were not far away, they fled. Fighting continued in the Vladař mountains throughout the fall and led to a strategically important confrontation at Kutná Hora that December.

---

**1** Thomas A. Fudge, *The Crusade Against the Heretics* (Aldershot: Ashgate 2002), 93.

**2** Fudge, *Crusade Against the Heretics*, 138.

Žižka had lost his remaining good eye during a siege earlier that year. Undeterred, the old soldier relied on his understanding of Bohemian topography to continue the campaign. In his bitterly anti-Hussite chronicle, Aeneas Silvius Piccolomini commented, "These blind people (the Hussites) were delighted to follow a blind leader."[3] Žižka ended up trapped outside of the royalist stronghold of Kutná Hora on December 21, surrounded by Sigismund's army. After a pitched battle, Sigismund and his mercenary captain, Pipo Spano, had Žižka trapped in a hollow west of the city. The snow was deep, and the crusaders set up camp, with an overjoyed Sigismund prepared to finish the Hussites on the next day.

The main Czech chronicle, that of Laurence of Březova, ends at exactly this point. Frederick Heymann, in his masterful biography of Žižka, recreated what happened next. Žižka knew the geography of the area well, and being blind, did not feel that attacking in the dark was that bad an idea. He appears to have engaged his soldiers in a progressive bombardment up the hill, pushing the hufnitze a few yards forward, and then firing, stunning the encamped crusaders, and breaking their lines. Sigismund was left possessing Kutná Hora, but the Hussites had escaped. This battle remains a tactical milestone, the first known instance of the use of mobile artillery to push aside an opposing force. Sigismund floundered throughout the coming winter, losing an estimated twelve thousand soldiers in his running battle with Žižka. Martin V was encouraging. "We have no doubts about your Grace's willingness to move quickly, and zealously, in order to eradicate the Czech heresy, and that this holy task is foremost in your mind, and that you have no need to be admonished further in this respect," he began, in a letter that would demand that Sigismund launch a third crusade in the spring of 1422.

The Hussites were aware that without a crowned head, Bohemia was in a politically vulnerable position, but were

---

3 Fudge, *Crusade Against the Heretics*, 126.

absolutely unwilling to submit to Sigismund's rule. The most powerful kingdom in Europe, Poland–Lithuania, would have been the ideal ally, had King Władislaw been willing to commit himself to opposition to Sigismund. Władislaw initially voiced tepid support of the Hussites, but was soon negotiating with Sigismund, with the promise of non-interference in Bohemia should Sigismund be willing to return Silesia to Polish rule. A Czech embassy of four ambassadors travelled to Poland to address this but were captured by a German baron in Silesia. This angered both the emperor and the king, and the negotiations came to nothing. The king's nephew Sigismund Korybut announced his readiness to support the Czechs, but Władislaw remained cautious. Sigismund's disastrous winter campaign in Bohemia encouraged Władislaw to explore the possibilities Korybut's support of the Hussites suggested, and he permitted his nephew to enter Bohemia as his representative. So Korybut arrived in Prague just as tensions over Želivský's execution were high, and he worked hard to gain the cooperation of the Czech nobility. The Polish prince was committed to uniting the Hussites, and with the support of Žižka, he achieved enough to convince the nobles of Bohemia and Moravia to meet in Časlav in June 1422, where they agreed to recognize Korybut as designated prince-regent of Bohemia.

At first, Korybut's rule went well, especially in Prague and its allied cities. But despite his working relationship with Žižka, Tábor and the nascent Orebite movement chafed at his attempts at control. The Orebite movement was based in Hradec Králové in eastern Bohemia, led by Ambrose of Hradec, a radical critic of Rome. Unlike Biskupec, Ambrose was less taken with the apocalyptic vision that had animated Tábor. Orebites frequently found common cause with Tábor and remained the dominant Hussite force in eastern Bohemia. Žižka's ties to the Orebite nobles, serving a critical role in preserving his military power base, put him in an uncomfortable position with Korybut, who never gained Orebite support. The Želivský party and some Táborite leaders met in Prague in late September to engineer riots and a popular movement against Korybut. The prince responded quickly,

ending the attempted coup, but failing to resolve the growing division between Tábor and Prague. By mid-October, the
Elector Friedrich Hohenzollern of Brandenburg had begun
the third crusade Sigismund had promised earlier that year
by invading Bohemia across a very broad front. Friedrich
succeeded in ending a Hussite siege of Karlstejn castle, but
fighting proved inconclusive throughout the countryside.
Korybut attempted a diplomatic resolution with Friedrich, but
his terms would have divided the Elector from Sigismund. By
November, the crusade had sputtered to an end. Shortly after
the Táborite coup attempt, Žižka drops out of all the narratives, surfacing again only in early 1423 having broken mys-
teriously with Tábor. Biskupec's records suggest that Tábor
had begun to shift to a more radical, even Pickhart, position.
In the meantime, Korybut's mission to the Hussites had lost
its political utility for Władislaw, so he left Prague at the end
of 1422. His presence had enabled Władislaw to press Sigismund successfully for the territory in Silesia, so the Hussites
entered 1423 without a prospective king.

Žižka's forces dominated Bohemia throughout 1423. He
led the majority Táborite and Orebite forces to dramatic victory in Hořice in April against Czech Catholic soldiers, and
again in August at Strachův Dvůr, this time against Prague
Hussites. The insuperable divisions within the Hussite movement define the events that unfolded between April and
August. Korybut had appointed Diviš Bořek as ruler of Hradec
Králové, and Žižka cooperated with him at Hořice. Soon after,
Diviš appointed his brother Jetřich to rule in his place, so he
could fight in Moravia. The Orebites rejected Jetřich because
they had embraced Žižka's Military Ordinance, with which the
old general had recently restructured his forces. This ordinance organized the army into a system of ranks, delineated
basic rules for campaign and military justice, and demanded
a strict Christian moral purity of each soldier. Historians have
yet to find evidence of Jetřich actively colluding with Prague
Hussites, who took a very dim view of this ordinance, but Žižka's immediate break with Jetřich, and Diviš's speedy return
to Prague suggest this. Diviš led an army of Prague Hussites

towards Hradec Králové, and Žižka met him at Strachův Dvůr, where he butchered the Prague forces.

Žižka then moved south, actually leaving Bohemia for a time in late September 1423. There are stories of a Hussite invasion of Hungary, but this never happened. He may have wandered briefly through Austria before invading Moravia several weeks later. At this point, Prague Hussites had begun negotiations with Czech Catholic nobles at Kolin. There they agreed to a formal negotiation at St. Gallen, in hopes of finding sufficient grounds for a cooperative strike against Žižka. The collected Bohemian nobles were poised to organize a baronial oligarchy for the kingdom, of which Sigismund was deeply suspicious, so he forbade the Catholic nobles to participate, and the confederation collapsed. Žižka had marched back towards eastern Bohemia to defend himself, and the combined Catholic and Prague armies trapped him at Kostelec (u Křížků), twenty kilometres south-east of Prague, where they had him backed up to the Vltava river for several days. He managed to elude them and slipped away, but they caught up with him again several days later, on June 7 at Malešov, close to Kutna Horá and Čáslav. This time, Žižka made excellent tactical use of his position on the heights above the town, and resoundingly defeated the allied forces, killing close to fourteen hundred soldiers of the Prague army.

Malešov was Žižka's final great victory. Had he been defeated, the Hussite movement would likely have ended soon thereafter. Instead, Žižka established his absolute control over all eastern Bohemia. Matters concluded when Žižka moved towards Prague, which he threatened in September 1424. Korybut, who had recently returned to Prague, managed to reconcile the Prague nobles with Žižka, thereby forestalling what would almost certainly have been the sack of the city. The victorious Žižka then marched towards Moravia, and stopped to lay siege to the castle of Přibyslav around October 7. He became sick with what his contemporaries called plague, and died on October 11, 1424. He was buried at Hradec Králové, but his tomb was demolished two centuries later, in the midst of the chaos of the Thirty Years' War. The connection of Žižka to the Hussite movement has generally been so complete that the next ten years can seem like a completely different affair. For all the military skills of his successors, like Procop Holý, and for all the Hussite victories that would define the next decade, nobody had the charismatic power over soldiers that Žižka had. Indeed, Howard Kaminsky ends his history with Žižka's death, explaining that the history of the development of Tábor as a revolutionary and reformative process had ended. For Kaminsky, Hussitism was a revolutionary movement, from which Prague had turned with the murder of Želivský. The other major work in English, Heymann's biography of Žižka, naturally ends here as well. The only history to address the second half of the Hussite revolution available to English readers was written by F. M. Bartoš in 1966 and translated by John Klassen in 1985. Bartoš was the preeminent Czech historian of Hussitism of the first half of the twentieth century, and his interests were less ideologically directed than Kaminsky's.

## 1424 to 1435

Hussite internal relations had been strained before Žižka's death, but afterwards, they became poisonous. Přibram and Biskupec led delegations that had attempted to find some common ground about liturgy and worship in June 1423 at Konopistě, but failed. Another conference followed, this time in Prague that November, with the same results. The mistrust between Tábor and the Orebites in eastern Bohemia increased after Žižka's death, and the Prague Hussites again moved against the divided radical Hussites. Korybut's star was fading in Prague, given the division among the Bohemian nobles and the weak support Władzslaw provided from Poland.

Violence erupted in February 1425 when Táborite forces again threatened Prague. Without Žižka, they lacked the tactical wherewithal to sustain a cohesive attack, and were driven off by the Prague defenders. Tábor raided throughout Bohemia for the rest of the year, achieving little beyond widespread destruction and suffering. In the meantime, Prague

Hussite nobles again met with Sigismund's delegation in Brno to find some grounds for alliance, with no success. This eventually brought Prague and Tábor back together, and following more fighting against Sigismund that September, they hammered out a peace accord at Vršovice, near Prague, on October 17, 1425. The treaty stipulated a governing council for the Hussite movement of twelve elected representatives, six from Prague and six from Tábor. Oreb lacked representation, which boded ill for the future of the treaty. Korybut was given leadership of the combined forces, and they spent the next two months fighting Catholics throughout Bohemia. Tábor and Oreb cooperated, but neither group could stomach Korybut as their leader.

Martin V appointed Cardinal Giordano Orsini to lead the papal effort to eradicate the Hussites, and Orsini, an experienced prosecutor of internal threats to orthodoxy, organized another crusade. Under the command of Boso of Fictum, an immense army of Saxons moved to Ústi nad Leben, in the mountains halfway between Dresden and Prague. Korybut led the Prague contingent, while Jan Rohač led the Orebites and Procop Holý led Tábor. On June 16, 1426, the Hussites resoundingly defeated the Saxons, one of the largest armies the church had yet sent into Bohemia. On his return to Prague, Korybut established regular diplomatic contact with Sigismund, which angered Tábor and Oreb. Worse, Korybut welcomed the support of Hynek of Poděbrady, long an enemy of Oreb, so Hynek soon found his castle surrounded by Táborites and Orebites. The siege failed, and Hynek rode out proudly, prepared to take violent revenge on a nearby Táborite town. As he rode through the castle gate, the massive iron portcullis slammed down on him, killing him instantly. The fortress reverted to his brother, upon whose death a year later, it became the property of the seven-year-old Jiři Poděbrady, the eventual king of Bohemia.

Korybut, possibly prompted by Sigismund, sent out peace feelers to Orsini, who refused to grant the Hussites a hearing. So he tried Poland, and his uncle Władyslaw sent word to Martin V of Korybut's willingness to compromise. Martin V responded warmly and, when word of this reached Prague, the barely healed divisions within the nobles and people burst open again. Jan Příbram, long the conservative voice among the Hussite theologians, was overjoyed at the prospect of an end to Wycliffism, and launched a campaign of preaching and disputations against Peter Payne and Jakoubek. Jakoubek responded in a sermon at Bethlehem chapel on December 22, 1426, angrily condemning Příbram and the papal letter. By March 1427, Prague was again at the point of violence because of the division between the two parties, with Korybut naturally supporting Příbram's side. Foolishly, Korybut imagined that things were sufficiently disorganized for him to invite Silesian nobles to invest the town and eliminate the Jakoubek wing of the Hussites. He sent two officials to notify his commanders to begin movement against the city, but the officials instead brought the orders to Jan Rokycana and the city council. Korybut was quickly overthrown, and was lucky to escape Prague alive, never to return.

For every "Great Battle" defining a season of war, opposed forces generally spend enormous amounts of time and energy manoeuvring from place to place, or in minor raids. After the Hussite triumph at Ústi in 1426, and Korybut's ouster in 1427, the conflict entered a period of relative calm. Sigismund had been occupied in defending the empire's Hungarian territory against the Turks, so Elector Friedrich of Brandenburg took it upon himself to organize a fourth crusade beginning on June 29, 1427. He planned for four armies attacking Bohemia from four different areas, the success of which depended on coordinated action and regular communication between the forces. First, though, he sent a letter to all concerned, including the Hussites in Prague, announcing his intentions. Since Korybut's departure, Příbram's conservatives were in decline and Jan Rokycana had gained influence. Tábor and Oreb were raiding in Silesia that May and June, so when Friedrich's letter arrived, Rokycana politely acknowledged it and did nothing further.

Friedrich had hopes of commanding this crusade, but Martin V selected Cardinal Henry Beaufort instead. The choice was reasonable. Henry, a son of John of Gaunt and an experienced soldier, arrived at Naumburg that June, but did little to direct the crusaders over the next month. The four forces blundered about until they reached Stříbro, to which they laid siege for a time, after which they moved to Tachov that August. Beaufort took command there, and stationed his forces in the fortress. Tachov had resisted Žižka in 1421, and proudly boasted possession of a giant bombard they named Chmelik. The Hussites surrounded Tachov, tunnelled under the walls, and took the fortress on August 11, 1427. They did not bother to take the bombard, though, preferring a smaller, more portable weapon.

While the fourth crusade did not end at Tachov, it had run out of steam. Beaufort called for a meeting of the crusading nobles to strategize, while Tábor and Oreb began a series of raids (*chevauchées* or "magnificent rides") into parts of Germany and Austria, as well as Silesia and Lusatia. The objective in such raids was plunder and the hope that the Slav minority in these areas would join their cause. Sigismund and Friedrich decided to try a different approach, given the emperor's ongoing commitment to fighting in Hungary. They managed to convince Procop Holý that negotiations were likely to yield promising results, and all agreed to meet on January 1, 1429 at Český Brod. Sigismund's diplomats made it clear that the emperor would be gentle with the rebellious Bohemians so long as they gave up their misguided theology, and Peter Payne, the Hussite spokesman, responded that they would welcome Sigismund's leadership should he be willing to accept the Four Articles of Prague. The result was deadlock, so Sigismund suggested that another meeting might be fruitful, this time on March 6 at Moravský Krumlov. The Hussites appeared, but Sigismund decided that such a conference might be better in a more neutral territory, and all agreed to a meeting in Bratislava on April 3.

The negotiations at Bratislava began well. Procop Holý and Peter Payne led the Hussite delegation, while a large group of Catholic nobles and university leaders from across Europe accompanied Sigismund. Payne presented the Hussite position, arguing that while the emperor was certainly convinced that he was serving God, he was deceived, the evidence for which was his repeated defeats at the hands of peasants. Sigismund responded that Henry Beaufort and other cardinals were preparing an ecumenical conference in Basel to begin in two years. Perhaps a truce could be arranged until all could meet at this conference? Neither side could imagine giving in to the other, so the Hussites composed a polite but firm letter defending the Four Articles and requested that the emperor rethink his request. Sigismund lost his patience, and negotiations ended with plans for a new crusade in June 1429.

Sigismund's council pressed for continued negotiations, so all met again in late May at the Clementinum in Prague. This lasted for several months, and ended with the Orebites and half of the Prague Hussites walking out when Sigismund requested that the Hussites return the land and wealth they had plundered, give up the castles they had captured, and extend the acting truce. For a time it looked as though the talks might still have succeeded, but Jakoubek died on August 4 and the Prague moderate forces lost their influence over the radical elements. By mid-August, talks had dwindled to a halt. But the divisions the talks had exposed as lasting within the Hussite movement erupted that month, and were kept from becoming violent only with the promise of extended talks over the coming two months. The theological disputes were headed by Jan Příbram and Peter Payne, and went nowhere, since each leader had become deaf to his opponent's arguments. Jan Rokycana was able to demonstrate his mediating abilities, and the talks were perceived as not without merit, so the archbishop of Prague made him acting head of the Prague clergy.

Both sides continued to undermine one another with inflammatory pamphlets and angry meetings. Tábor published a treatise extolling Jakoubek's Eucharistic theology, which denied transubstantiation, and Příbram responded with a broadside against Procop Holý. This was the tipping point for many in Prague, and Příbram had to leave Prague, not to return for nine years. The latter part of 1429 found the Orebites defeated in Lusatia and Silesia, while Tábor met with some success in these regions. At year's end, Prague, Oreb, and Tábor united to attack Saxony in what would be known as the Glorious Campaign of 1430. The Saxon army was powerful but failed to meet the Hussites in the field. Instead, the Hussites led them on a chase through Saxony and Franconia. Eventually, on February 10, 1430, John Elector of the Palatinate signed a peace treaty with the victorious Hussites at Beheimstein castle near the western border of Bohemia. Part of the peace treaty involved free passage for Hussite preachers to Naumburg, where they would be allowed to proselytize in April. Not surprisingly, the details of planning such a program became impossible to manage, so Elector Friedrich offered to send a letter to Sigismund on behalf of negotiating peace. This led to plans for a formal meeting at Cheb, but these came to nothing.

Tábor published a unique pronouncement in German declaring willingness to meet and talk with church authorities.

> If the pope and the entire clergy have truth, there is no doubt they will be superior to us and will defeat us with the word of God. However, if they are on the side of lies, it will be impossible to prove their conviction and intention. For this reason, beloved and sincere people and lords, rich and poor, we exhort you and all Imperial cities together with the king, dukes, and the lords in the name of divine justice to come to a written agreement among yourselves for a day of negotiation which shall be certain and opportune for you and us. At this time you may bring your bishops and scholars, and we will bring our scholars. We will permit them to do battle using the word of God before all of us and no one shall triumph using violence and cunning, but shall only use the word of God! If your bishops and doctors demonstrate the superiority of their faith from Holy Scripture and our faith pronounced unrighteous in that case we will desire to correct ourselves and repent according to the Holy Gospel. On the other hand, if your doctors and bishops are the ones defeated with reasoning from the Holy Scriptures, then in that case, you will repent and unite with us and remain with us.[4]

---

4 Fudge, *Crusade Against the Heretics*, 287.

While the new year found Tábor successful in raiding Moravia, Oreb ran into Sigismund's army as they entered Hungary and were seriously defeated. By June, though, Tábor and Oreb united in Moravia and moved into Silesia. Henry Beaufort had planned to lead Sigismund's armies against the Hussites in spring 1430, but had been called to fight the French in the campaign against Jean d'Arc. When she heard of the violence and destruction the Hussites had dealt throughout German-speaking lands, she was horrified and indignantly called for the Hussites to cease and desist.

> There is no perversity or cruelty which you have not entered into. You pollute the sacraments of the church, tear apart the articles of the faith, destroy churches, smash images of good remembrance, and kill Christians in order to maintain your faith. Where does your fury come from, or what obsession of rage drives you? [...] You are blind and not as those who have no eyes and cannot see. Do you really think that you shall escape punishment?[5]

Martin V had been working towards peace with the Hussites through another avenue since 1428. He had sent a papal nuncio to Kraków to make use of Władyslaw's relatively good relations with the Hussites, but internal divisions within Poland obstructed progress until 1430. Enough Polish nobles found the prospect of Sigismund's rule of Bohemia unpleasant that Władyslaw made a formal offer to the Hussites to host talks between them and the pope. But these quickly came to nothing in March 1431 thanks to the archbishop of Kraków's mistrust of the Bohemians. Few noticed in Prague, though, because a diet at Kutná Hora earlier that year had set in motion talks between Prague, Oreb, and Tábor. As usual, consensus was elusive, but Příbram's absence allowed Rokycana to set a less divisive tone to the proceedings, which Biskupec, representing the radical wing, reciprocated.

Sigismund and Friedrich sensed that the time was right for a shift in their approach to Bohemia after Martin V died

---

5 Fudge, *Crusade Against the Heretics*, 285.

on February 20, 1431. They were guided by the recently appointed papal legate, Cardinal Julian Cesarini, who began his call for crusade by promising to make use of all the funds everyone had already sent to Rome to pay for the past, failed crusades. Sigismund still hungered for the Bohemian crown and needed Cesarini's support to convince whomever was going to be the next pope of his claim to it. He had arranged for new peace talks at Cheb for May, but Cesarini sent his own delegates there, who guaranteed that the talks would fail. By June 28, Prague, Tábor, Oreb, and other allies of the Hussites had gathered near Plzeň and were waiting for the onslaught.

They waited for a month as Elector Friedrich, his own army camped on the Bohemian border, made one last attempt at negotiations. He received the customary refusal to abandon the Four Articles on July 21, and six days later, Cesarini fired back with a question: How could faithful Christians trust Bohemian nobles and false clergy rather than the Church and her God given authority? No answer was expected, and the crusaders entered south-western Bohemia on August 1. The Hussites withdrew to the fortress of Tachov, and the crusaders began a siege. John Count Palatine, one of the crusaders' leaders, had long had his eye on that fortress, and prevented the bombardment that would have given the crusaders a chance at victory. So the crusaders abandoned the siege and took a page out of the Hussites' play book, pillaging and looting across south-west Bohemia for several weeks, until they arrived at the Táborite town of Domažlice on August 11.

Táborite messengers escaped the town and arrived at the Hussite camp at Tachov, and reinforcements began to march rapidly to Domažlice. Elector Friedrich recognized the need to find better ground, but Cesarini angrily refused to move. Friedrich constructed a small fortification for the cardinal on a nearby hill and began to organize his forces to move to a more defensible position. The Hussites arrived and tore into the jumble of mounted units and infantry, scattering the crusaders and forcing Cesarini to flee in fear of his life. Casualties at Domažlice were low, but the loot the crusaders had accumulated over the past several days was a welcome addition to Hussite coffers, and Cesarini's cardinal's hat was proudly displayed at Domažlice.

After Domažlice, Hussite military fortunes waned. Procop led the Táborites into Silesia while Čapek of Sány led into Moravia the *Sirotčí svaz* (or "Orphans Union" who had formerly followed Žižka under the Orebites). Both moved into Slovakia that September, but Procop grew nervous and turned back to Bohemia, which infuriated Čapek. Procop's intuition had been sound. A large Hungarian army found the Orphans in November, and chased them tirelessly through the rough country of the Slovak Moravian frontier. The Orphans marched, exhausted and freezing for a month in an ordeal remembered as the Hussite Anabasis. Čapek angrily blamed Procop for abandoning him, and the radical wing was divided. Tábor had likewise suffered humiliating defeats in the south, stumbling upon a powerful Austrian force, which thrashed them at Weidhoffen. As 1431 came to an end, Sigismund's invitation to meet at council in Basel provided a good reason for the three Hussite factions to reconsider their differences. In Prague's Old Town, representatives gathered from February 10 to 27, 1432 to build consensus for a possible delegation to Basel. Procop and Čapek resolved their differences, thus temporarily uniting Tábor and Oreb. In the end, the Prague leaders sent a letter back to Sigismund accepting his invitation to Basel, and requested a series of talks at Cheb, to begin in May. In the meantime, the Táborites and the Orphans spent that spring raiding in Lusatia and Silesia, as had become the Hussite custom.

The ecumenical church council at Basel had begun that summer, and the Hussite problem was a major concern. The members were divided about meeting with them until Cesarini arrived in September and convinced the council that formal talks were likely to yield more success than military force. The new pope Eugenius IV did not agree, though, and attempted to dissolve the council while calling for yet another attack on the Hussites. Cesarini and Sigismund refused to obey the pope, and both supported the conciliarist resolve to continue. Eugene IV was opposed to Sigismund's coronation in Bohemia, so Sigismund had nothing to lose and everything to gain by supporting the council. But first, the Cheb negotiations, known as the Cheb Judge, had to produce groundwork for a Hussite delegation that might succeed in Basel.

All the previous negotiations between the Hussites and Sigismund had foundered on the issue of the Four Articles. The Hussites would not accept compromise downplaying Scripture's sovereignty and centrality, while the Catholic theologians refused to accept them defining Scriptural truth. At Cheb, both sides eventually agreed upon a carefully worded compromise. "In the dispute about the Four Articles which the Bohemians advocate, the Law of God and the practice of Christ, the apostles, and the primitive church, together with the councils and doctors truly founded on this practice, shall be accepted at the Council of Basel as the truest and indisputable judge." Both the conservative Catholics and the radical Hussites bit their tongues at this, while the moderate elements on both sides prevailed. Politically, the Czechs were understandably chary regarding the promise of self-passage, given what had happened with Hus at Konstanz. With careful negotiations, the Hussites dropped their demands for hostages, and incredibly, the Imperial delegation agreed not to demand a general truce for the duration of the council. The spirit of compromise at Cheb was reason for hope in the midst of very violent times.

Hussite raiders spent the summer in Silesia and Moravia, and their generals travelled to Poland. The king had decided to attack the Teutonic Knights, and needed as many allies as he could find. Not all the Hussites were happy with this possibility. Hadn't Sigismund showed good faith as a prospective ruler by facilitating negotiations at Basel? Another diet at Kutná Hora in September narrowly approved of the alliance, and separate truces with Lusatia, Silesia, and Saxony were established. The general spirit of harmony from Cheb seemed to hold between the Hussite parties at year's end. 1432 had been remarkable in that the Hussites had reached agreement in Prague in February, the meeting to prepare for the meeting to prepare for Basel. Then again at Cheb, the meeting to prepare for the meeting at Basel, the Hussites and the Emperor found common ground. Finally, at Kutná Hora, the meeting to finish preparing for the meeting at Basel, the Hussite parties again managed compromise. Hopes were high as the delegation travelled to Basel in January 1433.

Fifteen delegates represented the Hussites at Basel, including Procop, Rokycana, Biskupec, and Peter Payne. This was a unique opportunity for all concerned, because the Bohemians found themselves the centre of attention in one of Europe's most cosmopolitan cities, while delegates from many countries had the chance to meet the leaders of the forces they had been fighting for the past twelve years. Cesarini and Procop met together for the first time on January 8 at a private dinner, but there is no record of talk of the cardinal's new hat. Contact between the Hussites and the local laity was carefully restricted, for fear of the heretical contagion the council feared would certainly spread with the Bohemians' arrival.

The proceedings began with the Hussite leaders defending the Four Articles, and the council's theologians providing carefully constructed refutations. After both sides had managed to address the issues more often than indulging in *ad hominem*, or worse *ad baculum*, comments, the time arrived for serious disputation. Biskupec faced Giles Charlier, nephew of Jean Gerson, in an extended argument about the legitimacy of capital punishment in Christian society. Biskupec was firmly opposed and accused the church of having made a foul compromise with the secular world in admitting its use. Petr Chelčický, who would eventually inspire a new movement from the ashes of Tábor, had known Biskupec, and the two struggled to find common ground. This topic was promising, and Chelčický would later use Biskupec's arguments in his own writings.

For many, the main event came when Peter Payne opposed Juan Palomar, a long-time critic of the Hussites. The topic was the article condemning clerical ownership of property. In his presentation, Payne was very careful to avoid mentioning John Wyclif's works, knowing full well that the Oxford don had been hereticated, and could not conceivably be regarded as a respectable authority. So he cited Archbishop Richard FitzRalph, whose *De pauperie Salvatoris* had strongly influenced the political thought of Wyclif instead. Or at any rate, he appeared to cite FitzRalph; in fact, he was citing Wyclif and claiming it to have been the work of FitzRalph. Payne was initially respectful of his opponent, but soon took to playing to the audience with playful asides and caustic rejoinders to Palomar's objections. The English delegation claimed that Payne had been excommunicated and declared a traitor in England, and so ought not be heard. Rokycana defended Payne to the council, and the matter came to a rest.

By March, it looked as though the arguments had arrived at their usual impasse. Nicholas of Cusa, a pupil of Cesarini and one of fifteenth-century Europe's greatest thinkers, wrote his *De concordantia catholica* about this time, and suggested the formation of a select committee to achieve some kind of positive result of the Hussite appearance at Basel. The church offered the Bohemians full participation in the Catholic community, provided they surrender the commitment to put the Bible before ecclesiastical authority. This effectively would have compelled the Hussites to forswear the Four Articles. The Hussites refused, so all agreed to another meeting to continue talks in Prague in April. With that, the Hussites left Basel, unwilling to wait for Sigismund to arrive. Cesarini politely expressed the council's thanks for peaceful and civil negotiations, and several others surreptitiously communicated sympathy with the Utraquist ideal to Rokycana, who by now was the acknowledged Hussite theological leader.

When the delegates met at the Clementinum in Prague on June 12, it became clear that a change of venue was not going to help matters. Juan Palomar led the council's delegation, and opened with the demand that the Hussites surrender all they had gained at Cheb, which meant burying the Four Articles. Naturally, Rokycana refused courteously, while Procop was more pointed. "Many obdurate enemies of the sacred Four Articles have in the end, through word and deed, affirmed their faith in them, and become willing to defend them to the death." Palomar began an angry response but appears to have realized that this was likely not the best place to assume the upper hand. Employing a time-honoured tactic, he suggested forming a committee to sort through the political details impeding compromise.

Enough council delegates recognized the conservative Hussite readiness to continue in pursuit of reconciliation that they agreed to accept the Utraquist position provided the Hussites dropped the other three articles. This pleased the conservative Hussites, and annoyed Oreb and Tábor. Palomar worked to expand this division within the Czechs and was less than subtle in his manoeuvring. The Hussite nobles perceived this and came down on the side of internal unity. The Basel delegates were satisfied that they had something to bring back to the council and prepared to leave. Before they left, several Hussite nobles, among them Menhart of Hradec, met with them to strategize about the coming months. All could see that the division between the Prague Hussites and the radicals in Tábor and Oreb was increasingly hampering Hussite success. The time was almost ripe to utilize this division to put an end to the movement.

Tábor had been casting about for a suitable place to raid that summer. The many truces following from Cheb reduced their options, so they settled on laying siege to Plzeň, ninety kilometres south-west of Prague. Plzeň had been subject to Táborite siege twice already, but had not fallen. The third siege began on July 13. The Orphans had been expected to join Tábor, but the treaty the Hussites had with Poland compelled them to march north to join the fight against the Teutonic Knights. The Poles and the Orphans at first tried to take the massive stronghold at Chojnice, but failed, so they moved towards Gdańsk. The fortress of Tczew was the port city's main defence, and it quickly fell. The city itself was a different matter and withstood repeated assaults. Čapek, leader of the Czech forces, declared victory and all enjoyed a beach celebration on the shores of the Baltic.

Catholic Plzeň was not yielding to Táborite attacks. The assembled delegates at Basel were watching this very carefully, increasingly identifying Plzeň as the Catholic stronghold of western Bohemia. Táborite supplies were dwindling, so two Táborite captains led a thousand men into Bavaria to resupply. They were ambushed by German troops, and suffered a crippling defeat. The two captains managed to return to the siege and began to campaign against Procop's leadership. In short order, Procop was overthrown, and ignominiously ejected from command. At the council, Jan Přibram and Procop of Plzeň, leaders of the conservative Hussite faction, worked together with the delegation returning from the Clementinum to convince the council to accept utraquism. This would be a challenge, because the chalice had been emblematic of the Hussite cause since 1415. After several weeks of argument, the council managed to formulate a position that was very much to their advantage. The issue of lay access to the chalice had always been open to theological discussion, they explained, so long as it followed the proper protocols. The Hussite presumption to define themselves by proclaiming its introduction exhibited a complete misunderstanding of the structure of Church decision-making, so the Konstanz theologians had quite rightly prohibited the lay chalice in 1415. Now the proper discussions had led the church to permit those Czechs *who accepted all other sacraments and rites of the faith* access to the chalice. The council knew that this formulation was certain to further divide the Hussite factions, since the conservatives would accept it, while Tábor and Oreb would reject it. With the fall of Procop and the failure of the Plzeň siege, prospects for Hussite unity were gloomy.

Representations from the three Hussite parties met with the Basel delegation again in November in Prague. Menhart of Hradec, who had earlier mapped out these events with the Basel delegates, took control of the November diet and invoked the agreement from the 1421 Časlav diet in which an acting regent and a council of advisors would guide the discussion. Aleš Vřeštovský, a respected Orebite leader, was elected. Aleš, likely guided by Menhart, compelled the more radical Hussites to accept the council's compromise. As talks continued, the Hussites gradually realized that accepting this compromise would certainly lead to the dispersal of the armies now in the field, and an end to the Hussite military dominance of the Czech lands. This was essentially a surrender disguised as a mutually beneficial compromise. The Hussites sent a delegate back to Basel with the counter offer: allow universal access to the lay chalice before an end to the hostilities, or there would be no end to the hostilities. The council predictably rejected this, and 1434 began with a universal dread that two years of talks had amounted to relatively little. Events would prove otherwise. During discussions the previous winter of 1433, the attempt at compromise included a rewritten version of the Articles that both sides described as a Compactata. When the Hussite delegates left Basel, they publicized this Compactata at Jihlava in 1436. This version of the Compactata would become the keystone for all further negotiations both within the Utraquist movement, and with popes and crowned heads for years to come, until 1567. Its articles are versions of the 1421 articles: the Utraquist version of Eucharist be available to those who desire it, all mortal sins should be punished, corrected, and eliminated, that the word of God be preached by capable priests and clerics, and that the clergy may not exercise the right of property ownership over temporal goods. The wording remained open for debate, and it would continue to evolve, but the Compactata had somehow managed to emerge from Basel as the groundwork for unification of the Utraquist movement.

Tábor had attacked Plzeň, the large Catholic stronghold, in July 1433, but the city was well defended, and a siege began. It lasted through to April 1434, when both sides were at the point of exhaustion. That January of 1434, after the Prague delegates had departed from Basel, the council sent Juan Palomar to attempt to find a diplomatic solution to the theological standoff. Palomar was a skilled diplomat and was ready to find consensus where there appeared to be no grounds for it. He wisely played on the old antagonism between Tábor and Prague, pointing out that the return of warfare to Bohemia was thanks to Tábor, certain to bring misery to Catholic and Hussite alike. He managed to construct an alliance between the Prague Hussite nobles and their Catholic counterparts that appeared ready to withstand the opposition of Tábor. Just as the Plzeň siege was about to come to what looked like a successful resolution for Tábor, the newly united allies took over Prague, expelling the Táborites who were dominant in the New Town which shocked the Táborite forces in Plzeň. In desperation, they appealed to Prokop Holy to take command, and marched from Plzeň towards Prague. In the meantime, troops under the newly allied lords had arrived in Prague and began to march to meet the Táborites. They met and the Táborites occupied a hill near Lipany, while the allied forces made camp by the river Hřib, facing them. It was clear that, at best, this would be the beginning of the end for Tábor, because even a victory would leave them so weakened as to make them easily overcome by another allied army. The battle of Lipany on May 30, 1434 turned on the Táborites mistaking the allied army's repositioning as the beginning of a rout. Gunfire had been so intense that smoke made visibility limited, so the mistake was understandable. When the Táborites attacked, the assembled cavalry and infantry met them directly and destroyed them. The killing lasted well into the evening, and among the many dead were Prokop Holý. Tábor was now finished as a military power.

The joyous Catholic reaction contrasted with the ambivalence the Prague Utraquists felt for the end of Tábor; however many arguments that had separated them, they had shared a common cause and had achieved much together. So as the danger to Plzeň receded and the Catholic celebrations continued, the alliance began to cool. The Hussite lords now recognized the magnitude of the task ahead. They would have to negotiate restitution of property, prevent the renewal of violence from Táborite or Orebite factions, and begin to reconstruct relations with the Catholic nobility, the Empire, and the Church, all the while maintaining their Utraquist identity.

Sigismund was more than ready to play his part and take the Bohemian throne, to which Rokycana agreed, so long as the Council of Basel agreed to recognize the Utraquist position as legitimate in the kingdom. This was certainly not an option so far as the council was concerned, so the throne would remain empty. By that fall it became evident that the peace they had welcomed in June could only continue if the Hussites renewed negotiations with council and Sigismund. The same frustrating ordeal of diets, special meetings, committees, and formal discussion followed, this time between Prague and the Catholics, rather than between Prague and Tábor. As this process dragged on through 1435, Sigismund achieved the small victory of outliving Korybut, who had joined the Poles in one of their wars with the Teutonic Knights and been captured and executed. This was balanced, though, by the Hussites electing Rokycana archbishop of the Utraquist church. Sigismund had to admit to the furious council that he had given theoretical approval to this in Brno, and had failed in his attempts to forestall it by having Rokycana murdered.

Another council between both Utraquist and Catholic Czechs and the council occurred in Hungary in late 1435, which ended the next January with the news that everyone agreed to meet that summer in Moravia for more talks. At this meeting, held in June in Jihlava, things appeared to be proceeding as usual, with proud exclamations, angry accusations, and angry bickering leading to the usual impasse, when, incredibly, the Compactata constructed at Basel in 1433 was found acceptable to both Catholic and Utraquist parties. Leaving aside the council's refusal to recognize Rokycana as archbishop, the way was now clear for Bohemia to accept Sigismund's coronation.

When Sigismund died in 1437, the political balance that had remained in Bohemia vanished. The designated heir, Albert of Habsburg, appealed to the Catholic nobles, and some moderate Prague Hussites, but the remaining Orebites and Táborites, still a political force, wanted Prince Casimir of Poland. Albert was crowned in Prague in June 1438, but not by Archbisop Rokycana, who had not been recognized by the pope. Instead, the Bohemian nobles and the bishop of Olomouc crowned him, thereby signifying a combination of having inherited the throne, and the approval of both Bohemian and Moravian authorities. After brief hostilities broke out between advocates of Casimir and Albert's forces, in which Albert prevailed, the new king departed for war with the Turks, and died of dysentery in 1439. His son, Ladislas, had been born five months after Albert's death, earning him the sobriquet Ladislas the Posthumous. He could hardly be crowned at that age, so the throne seemed doomed to remain empty. In June 1440, thirty-seven electors were selected to find a candidate for the crown, and Albrecht III of Bavaria was approached. He declined the offer. The throne would remain empty for the duration of Ladislas's minority.

Incredibly, a mutual recognition that the Compactata of 1436 provided a stable basis for agreement throughout Bohemia and Moravia allowed the kingdom to remain comparatively viable throughout the 1440s. A Táborite minority continued to reject the Compactata, and the pope had never recognized it, but the Basel Council remained sufficiently authoritative as to ensure its legitimacy for the purposes of internal and external politics. In 1448, the papal legate Juan Caraval visited Prague, and demanded both Burgrave Menhart of Hradec and Papošek of Soběslav, the Utraquist leader, to revoke the Compactata. Once again, the tottering structure of political order seemed ready to collapse. The young noble Jiři of Poděbrady unified some of the Bohemian nobles and knights into a union and occupied Prague. He recalled Rokycana from his exile, and overthrew Menhart and Papošek, foiling the papal attempt at overthrowing the Compactata. By the end of the year, the danger had passed, and Jiři was established as Land Administrator for Bohemia. By 1453, Jiři and Rokycana had stabilized the kingdom, making it possible to crown Ladislas, now fourteen, without fear of a threat to his authority. Ladislas died three years later, and in 1458, Jiři was elected king of Bohemia. Precedent for such an election had been set in neighbouring Hungary, when Matthias Corvinus was elected to the throne in 1457. Bohemia now had a Hussite king.

While Jiři Poděbrady was prepared to rule a kingdom that was both Catholic and Hussite, the pope had other ideas.

Aeneas Silvius Piccolomini, now Pius II, had familiarity with the Hussites, having visited them, argued with them, and been infuriated by them in 1451. When Jiři was crowned, Pius completed his *Historica Bohemica*, a deeply partisan account of the Hussites that continues to infuriate some Czechs and amuse its other readers. Jiři attempted to forestall papal condemnations by marrying his daughter to Matthias Corvinus in 1461, but in March 1462 Pius condemned the Compactata anyway, and threatened other kingdoms with dire punishment for any apparent support of Hussite ideas. Jiři responded by proposing an association of European rulers that could be the basis for an EU-style congress of nations. The French king Louis XI ridiculed the idea, and Jiři found no other potential allies.

When Pius died in 1464, and Jiři's daughter died shortly afterwards, it became even more difficult to hold onto the Bohemian crown. The new pope, Paul II, increased pressure on Bohemian Catholic nobles to oppose Jiři, and in November the nobles responded by forming the Zelenohorská Union. By 1467, the Union and Jiři were engaged in combat, and a second Hussite war had begun. Fighting raged through the Czech lands, and Matthias Corvinus, with his eye on expanding his kingdom northwards, joined the Union in 1468. This changed matters. Matthias had long experience leading armies against the Turks, and soon had control of Moravia and western Bohemia. He met with Jiři to discuss the possibility of peaceful resolution in early 1469, but the fighting continued. Within a few months the Union, and nobles from Lusatia and Silesia, proclaimed Matthias king of Bohemia. Jiři's health had begun to decline, and his supporters had hoped that the Polish crown would send an heir to take the Hussite king's place, but the Jagellonians showed little interest in that possibility. Jiři's army invaded Moravia in 1470, but both sides quickly found themselves both militarily and financially exhausted. After a year of weary stand-off, Jiři died in March 1471, and it seemed that the Czech lands had fallen into the same terrible state they had occupied fifty years before.

Jiři had convinced his loyal nobles to elect Vladislaus, eldest son of Casimir IV Jagellion of Poland, to follow him.

After Vladislaus agreed to respect the coherence of a state with two valid species of Christianity, he was elected at a Diet at Kutná Hora in 1471. In short order, Vladislaus was at war with Matthias Corvinus, which lasted until they met at Olomouc in 1479 in mutual recognition that both sides had achieved little beyond deadlock. They agreed to allow Moravia to remain Catholic and Bohemia to continue with its two alternatives. The pope remained opposed to Bohemia's recognition of utraquism, so Vladislaus, hoping to regain some papal approval, attempted to replace Utraquist town councils with Catholic ones. The immediate result was an uprising in Prague in September 1483, convincing Vladislaus that his reign's success owed more to the cooperation of his subjects than to the possibility of papal approval.

So in March 1485, another diet convened at Kutná Hora to formalize the place of the Compactata as the law of all Bohemia, permitting each community to define itself as either Catholic or Utraquist, as it chose. Note that the dominant nobles' opinion played no role here. If the local nobility of a town was Utraquist, but the townspeople were Catholic, the town would be Catholic. In 1434, when the Council of Basel had agreed to the implementation of the Compactata throughout Bohemia to achieve peace, the intent had been to gradually cut off acceptance of utraquism. Fifty-one years later, it was clear that the strategy had failed.

The odd group out was the *Unitas fratrum*. While closer to the Utraquists than to the Catholics, their pacifism and moralistic zeal set them apart. By the 1480s, an interest in developing their strictly biblical approach into a more complex articulation of their version of a reformed church arose. Luke of Prague (d. 1511) was a university trained theologian who gravitated to the *Unitas fratrum* in 1481, saw this need, and began to develop a more sophisticated theological vision. The Brethren had formally organized themselves in the Rýchnov Mountains in 1464, led by Řehoř (Gregory), a nephew of Rokycana and had incorporated several other small groups, including former Táborites, Adamites, and some Waldensians. Following the teachings of Chelčický, the Brethren had been primarily an orthopraxic movement, concerned with living the Christian life rather than defining its formal ideals. During the Second Hussite War between Jiři and Matthias in 1467–1468, the Brethren had refused to take up arms in defence of Bohemia, earning Jiři's enmity. They grew in numbers, and by Řehoř's death in 1474, had become a moderately sized minority within the Utraquist fold. When Luke of Prague began to attract some like-minded followers in favour of a better developed theology, a schism appeared within the movement. A minority party, known as the Minors, rejected the intellectualizing of formal theology, while the larger party (known as the Major party; not, as the Franciscans, the Conventuals) were prepared to follow Luke. In a synod in 1495, the Major party won out, and Luke continued as the leader until his death in 1511. In later years, he corresponded with Luther, who regarded him distastefully as leader of the Pickhart heresy. Luther's position would change, however, after a debate with Eck in 1519.

In 1490 Vladislaus had manoeuvred himself onto the Hungarian throne, succeeding Matthias and leaving Bohemia in the hands of several trustworthy nobles. While he lived until 1516, Vladislaus's attentions shifted towards Hungary and later towards war with the Ottoman Turks. By then, Luther's ninety-five theses were set to touch off the events that led to the Protestant Reformation in Germany. As mentioned, Luther had scant regard for what he understood of Hussitism for some years. "When I was a papist, I truly and cordially hated these Pickard Brethren [...]. When I came upon some books of John Hus unawares one time and saw that the Scriptures were treated so powerfully and purely [...] I immediately closed the book in terror, suspecting that there was a poison hidden under the honey by which my simplicity might be infected, such a violent fascination with the name of the pope and council ruled over me."[6]

---

**6** Quoted in Craig Atwood, *The Theology of the Czech Brethren from Hus to Comenius* (University Park: Pennsylvania State University Press, 2009), 246.

## Protestantism, Utraquism, and Bohemia

Initially the Utraquists were pleased to learn of Luther's ideas, but they quickly fell into the usual divide between radicals and conservatives. Recognizing that Luther's reform was leading to an irrevocable break with Rome, the conservative Utraquists edged away from Luther, while the radical party embraced him. At the same time, a surprisingly large number of the German-speaking inhabitants of the Czech lands, long-time opponents of utraquism, decided that Luther was probably right. The situation of the Brethren was different; while Luke of Prague and Luther may initially have found common grounds, the differences between the two groups soon became too important to overlook. The Brethren rejected Luther's justification through faith, while Luther and his followers were sceptical of what they regarded as a too Roman understanding of Eucharist.

Ferdinand I was elected King of Bohemia in 1528, bringing the kingdom firmly into the Habsburg sphere of control. In German-speaking lands, fighting between Protestants and Catholics led to the Peace of Augsburg in 1555. This entailed a compromise by which the principle of *cuius regio, eius religio* allowed the ruler of a state to determine whether it would be Protestant or Catholic. This led to alarm in Bohemia, since Ferdinand was a firm supporter of Catholicism, while the kingdom was divided between Catholics, Lutherans, and Utraquists. Ferdinand died without resolving the issue in 1570, and was succeeded by Maximilian II, who was less interested in re-catholicizing the kingdom. The Lutherans and the Utraquists prepared the Bohemian Confession of 1575, which formulated the *status quo ante* as had been defined at Kutná Hora. Maximilian gave verbal approval of the document, but as a Catholic king, forbade its printing and publication.

The Catholic response to Protestantism had developed as a result of the Council of Trent, from 1545 to 1565. When Maximilian was succeeded by Rudolf II, it looked as though he would be less well inclined to Bohemian Protestantism. After all, he had been raised in the Spanish court. But his interests were wide ranging, eclectic, and sometimes simply odd, and he appears to have had little interest in the Counter-Reformation, beyond publishing the Letter of Majesty in 1609, which reiterated the standing arrangement of toleration of Protestantism in the kingdom. In the meantime, the Jesuits had begun work in Bohemia, founding a university and library at the Clementinum in Prague in 1522, and sending out teachers and priests into Bohemia and Moravia to counter the Utraquist and Lutheran theologies with education and convincing preaching. Rudolf abdicated and died in 1611, and was succeeded by his brother Matthias, who in turn was succeeded by Ferdinand II. Ferdinand was no friend to Protestantism and began to forbid the building of Protestant chapels on royal land. The Bohemian nobles protested against this in the national assembly, and Ferdinand dissolved it. Several from both Catholic and Protestant parties met in the Chancellory in Prague's New Town in May 1618 to discuss this. Tempers frayed, the conversation lurched into furious argument, and soon, two Catholic nobles were thrown out of the third-storey window. This was the Second Defenestration of Prague, from which both defenestrated nobles survived, but the peace that had held for over a century in Bohemia could not. Armies began to gather throughout Central Europe. Ferdinand II became Holy Roman Emperor in 1619, and the Bohemian nobles agreed to eject him from their throne, fearful that he would stamp out Protestantism in the kingdom. He did so at any rate, bringing his army into Bohemia and destroying the Bohemian forces at White Mountain on November 8, 1620. This inaugurated the disastrous Thirty Years' War, and defined the end of the Hussite movement in Bohemia.

# Chapter 3

# Hussites in History

The place of the Hussites in Czech history has always been a source of controversy. From the defeat at White Mountain in 1620 to the period following Napoleon's defeat of the Austro-Hungarian empire, the Hussites were regarded as heretics. Statues of emperors continue to dot the empire's cities featuring a snake or dragon being trampled under the imperial foot; in Czech lands, the identity of that serpent was Hussite. Today, travellers will encounter shrines and statues dedicated to St. John Nepomuk, a fourteenth-century priest famous for refusing to divulge the information the queen had confessed to him to an angry King Václav of Bohemia. He was thrown from the Charles bridge to his death, and after White Mountain, was promoted as the perfect replacement to overcome the hagiographic cult of Hus.

Among the first scholars to pay serious attention to Hus and Hussitism were German church historians who identified them as forerunners of Protestantism. Attempts to identify the Hussites with Czech nationalism were not desirable for the Habsburgs, though. The Catholic identity of the Empire suffered from Napoleon's invasion and the ignominious defeat at Austerlitz, not far from Brno. Enlightenment secularism remained a threat to the Empire's hold over populations either prone to Protestantism, Eastern Orthodoxy, or those sceptical of Roman Catholic dogma. But the drama the Hussites inspired among Romantic era authors and artists had the same effect among the Czech intelligentsia that tales of medieval Scotland had on writers like Sir Walter Scott. Perhaps the most famous of the non-Czech works of this period is George Sand's *Jean Ziska: Épisode de la guerre des Hussites*. She developed an interest in the subject during a trip through the Czech lands, and when she wrote, she explained that Žižka was a real person, despite the drama and energy that cast him as such a Romantic figure.

When Josef Jungmann published his massive Czech–German dictionary in 1834–1839, the Czech language was regarded as little better than a bucolic patois by the German-speaking upper and middle classes. One of the figures instrumental in publishing this dictionary was František Palacký, now regarded as the founder of modern Czech historiography. His editions of the documents of the Hussites, particularly the Chronicle of Lawrence of Březova in the fifth volume of his *Fontes rerum bohemicarum*, his edition of the documents of Hus's trial in 1869, and his own narrative of the Hussite war (*Urkindliche Beitrage zur Geschichte des Hussitenkriegs* in 1873) are the first important contributions to the modern recovery of the movement.

In the 1860s, Karl Adolf Constantin von Höfler characterized Germany as the instrument of Bohemian civilization, and Jan Hus as the Czech rejection of that gift. This rejection led directly to Kutná Hora and the flight of the German scholars from Prague University, thereby degrading the university for decades to come. Hus slavicized Bohemia, throwing away all that was excellent, and replacing it with weakness, fractiousness, and disorder. No wonder, he said, that Germanic peoples were destined to dominate the East—on their own, Slavs are capable of little. It was not until the Thirty Years' War, Höfler concluded, that Bohemia began to recover. Palacký responded to Höfler by demanding to know whether Hus had been right. Was the church corrupt and on the wrong path in the fifteenth century, as a comparison with the church described in the biblical Book of Acts would suggest, or were the curia and the bishops right to defend it? Palacký's Protestantism had led him to formulate his response, and he felt the answer was obvious. In switching the discussion from German

versus Czech to German and Roman versus Czech and Protestant, he formed the basis for a Czech nationalist argument
against the German *völkische* polemic. Palacký published a
somewhat refined version of his response in German, but his
original, Czech version contributed importantly to the creation of Hus as national martyr. Hus, Palacký explained, had
not been executed for heresy in Konstanz, but was murdered
by Imperial and Roman forces dedicated to maintaining control over the Czechs. Papal commands and legal obfuscation
pass for authoritative decision-making in the Catholic church,
while in Protestantism, specifically Czech Protestantism, the
simple clarity of reason is authority enough. Following this
line, Palacký describes Romans, Germans, Huns, and Mongols
as nations bent on taking what they can by force and subjugation, while the Jews, the Greeks, and the Slavs adopted the
ideal of freedom and forbearance from conquest.

Palacký was the first to formulate the Hussite movement as a true revolution, attempting to define a people by
freeing itself from subjugation and foreign domination. This
is not to downplay the theological elements of Hussitism.
Höfler, Palacký said, is the one responsible for doing that.
For Palacký, Protestantism is the other side of the coin of
national freedom, and the Catholicism of Imperial Vienna is
the obverse of the primitive oppression of Habsburg dominance. Palacký used Hus to catalyze the Czech Awakening,
which would rescue the Czech language from its desuetude,
and the folk-ways from the oblivion to which all too many con-
quered civilizations are consigned. This was a period when
European powers were becoming more centralized in the
1860s, and the smaller cultures were being swallowed by the
imperial beasts.

Höfler was only half arguing with Palacký *against* Czech
nationalism, while attempting to articulate the position of
the Sudeten Germans, who were living in large stretches of
Bohemia and Moravia. They were torn between the Prussian
nationalism on march to the north, and Austrian struggles
to maintain a coalition with Hungary in the south. By 1866,
Prussia and Austria would be at war with one another, which

ended quickly with Bismarck's victory at Hradec Králové that July. It was in the Viennese interests, represented by Höfler, to connect the Sudeten Germans with Catholic Austria rather than Protestant Prussia. Hence, Hus functioned within German-speaking lands as a threat to Austro-Hungarian imperial ambitions in the face of the ever increasing menace of Prussia. It was as if to suggest that division from within the Empire on the part of the Sudeten Germans could lead to the same chaos as the Bohemians had let loose four centuries earlier.

In the second half of the nineteenth century, Hus and Žižka rose to heroic stature in the populist nationalism that was growing in Czech lands. For example, 1868 saw a large number of Czech pilgrims travel to Konstanz to commemorate what was assumed to have been Hus's 500th birthday. A real estate developer and admirer of the Hussites built a residential district in an area of what was then suburban Prague, on the Vitkov hill. This hill, the site of Žižka's great victory in Prague, is now the Žižkov, and is one of the city's beautiful parks. Over the Žižkov, and overlooking the city and the river, lours the cyclopean equestrian statue of Jan Žižka, erected in January 1950. For about a decade, Žižka scowled from the Žižkov while a massive statue of Stalin did the same from an overlook at Letná Park. They both directed their gaze south, towards Tábor, which had become, through Enlightenment and Soviet histories, the heart of Hussitism.

Tábor had always been associated with the Hussites, but the Táborite unwillingness to accede to Catholic ideals maintained by the Prague Hussites struck a chord among Czech "Free Thinkers" in the late nineteenth century. It was illegal to be anything other than Catholic in the Austro-Hungarian Empire. The nationalist Young Czechs party regarded the Catholic church as one of the main guardians of Austrian domination, and its members became interested in the Free Thought movement then growing in Europe. This movement, associated with a broad spectrum of ideologies critical of the European social order, had regular World Congresses, and the gathering in Paris in 1905 featured a set of lectures on Ethics Without God that had a great effect on the Prague delegation.

The Young Czechs adopted this as a humanistic, democratic, socially critical alternative to Catholicism. In short order, people began to make connections to the Hussite nationalist imagery, especially the Táborites. Making the same mistake the Pickharts had made, late-nineteenth-century free thinking Czechs assumed that a group of communistic critics of Catholicism were probably religious sceptics as well.

The most dramatic evidence for the Young Czech zeal for Hussitism is another Prague landmark, the statue of Hus in Old Town Square. This was erected in 1915 to face the Marian column, which had been put up by the Habsburgs to commemorate the Catholic *reconquista* following the Thirty Years' War. This column was torn down shortly after the Armistice in 1918. The Hus statue remained a touchstone for Czech national identity during the Nazi and Soviet occupations, where people felt they were registering their humble votes of protest simply by sitting in its shadow.

Palacký and the Young Czechs had unyoked theology from the Hussite movement, substituting it with nationalism. The tension between Prague and Tábor seemed tailor made for the social conflict that had begun to develop in late-nineteenth-century Europe. Palacký had described that conflict in terms of the parties' differing attitudes towards Catholic authority, and as a Protestant himself, he identified the Táborites as embodying a greater zeal for freedom from hegemonic control. The shift away from portraying Tábor in theological terms to social and political ideologies continued in the use of Hussitism to inspire Czech nationalism at the turn of the twentieth century by Tomaš G. Masaryk, the founder and first president of Czechoslovakia. In his 1915 essay "Jan Hus and the Czech Reformation" he asks, "How can we Czechs belong to the Catholic church, yet acknowledge Hus as a national martyr, honour and revere him?" When he spoke, the majority of Czechs remained Roman Catholic, and were subjects of the Catholic Austro-Hungarian empire; Protestantism was very rare in the Czech lands, and the church now known as the Hussite church was not yet instituted. Masaryk answers, "Hus, the Táborites, Chelčický, and Komensky gave us a better, a higher form of religion than was given to us by the Roman theocracy." Further on in the essay, Masaryk contrasts Jan Žižka and the violent Táborite movement with Chelčický, and admits that, while he is fond of Žižka, and while he is impressed with Hus's example, he chooses Chelčický and his way of non-violence, just as he chooses Komensky and his way of harmonious education. "It thus seems to me that the present task of Czech men and women is to find a way of bridging Komensky and Chelčický."[1] Jan Patočka commented that Masaryk embraced a "puritanism, when man disciplines himself [...] he receives support from the absolute [...] an individual religion Masaryk concluded is ingrained in the Czech tradition, as with Hus and the Brethren, which is thoroughly nonscholastic, nontheological, above all, moral."[2] Masaryk continued with this line of questioning as he guided the Czech lands to nationhood. "Are we a nation of Žižka and Prokop, or of Hus and Komensky?"[3] Despite the occupation of Czechoslovakia in 1938, and its domination by the Soviets from 1948 to 1989, the Czech state remains Masaryk's creation. When he represented it to the world, he repeatedly proclaimed "Tábor is our program," meaning that it was not religion, but a social and political movement towards a new age. For Masaryk, the Hussites embody his post-Enlightenment humanist elevation of individual liberty in the face of hegemonic oppression, standing up to Pope and Emperor just as he and the Young Czechs had done against the Austro-Hungarian Empire.

Masaryk's interest in the fine points of Hussite theology was minimal, which infuriated the Czech historian Josef Pekař.

---

1 Tomáš G. Masaryk, *The Meaning of Czech History*, ed. Rene Wellek (Chapel Hill: University of North Carolina Press, 1974), 10–13.

2 Jan Patočka, "An Attempt at a Czech National Philosophy and Its Failure," in *T. G. Masaryk in Perspective: Comments and Criticisms*, ed. Milíč Čapek and Karel Hrubý (Ann Arbor: SVU, 1981), 8.

3 Tomáš G. Masaryk, *Ceská Otázka* (Prague: Svoboda, 1990), 184, my translation

Pekař is recognized as the foremost Czech historian of the first part of the twentieth century. His approach was much more scientific, more attentive to understanding the Hussite movement in its fifteenth-century context. His assessment included the Hussite phenomenon's social and economic effects on the Czech lands, and he argued forcefully that events must be understood as articulations of their age, not as realization of some philosophical ideology. He was just as suspicious of the Czech nationalist reading of the Hussites as he was of the growing Marxist interest, which had begun to evoke Hus and Tábor as forerunners of communism. Karl Kautsky described the development of Tábor as the force behind the rejection of the idea of private property. They may have described their ideology in theological terms, he admitted, but this was the language of thought of the period. They may have preached of apostolic poverty, but their meaning was to articulate a fundamental social materialism that lies at the base of the class struggle.

Kautsky's description set the tone for the post-Second World War Czech understanding of Hussitism. The post-war political and cultural figure, Zdeněk Nejedlý, was prepared to follow Kautsky, having rejected Palackýs nationalism and, struggling to find a middle ground between Pekař and Masaryk, he identified Hussitism as proto-Marxist, emphasizing Kautsky's rejection of theology as having real meaning in the movement. Peter Morée characterizes the post-war image of Hus, observing that "he might have marched in the streets with communists rather than preaching from the pulpit."[4] Nejedlý became minister of education in the new Soviet regime that began in 1948, and his vision quickly became

---

4 Peter Morée, "Not Preaching from the Pulpit but Marching in the Streets: The Communist Use of Hus," in *Bohemian Reformation and Religious Practice, Volume 6: Papers from the Sixth International Symposium on the Bohemian Reformation and Religious Practice*, ed. Zdenek V. David and David R. Holeton (Prague: Main Library, Czech Academy of Sciences, 2007), 283–96. Available from www. brrp.org. Accessed June 14, 2019.

an ideal vehicle to propagandize the populace. School children were compelled to learn of Hus and Žižka as the forefathers of the Soviet Czech state. President Klement Gottwald mocked Masaryk saying, "It is all very well for the bourgeoisie to maintain its hold on the state with 'Tábor is our program' for the program was issued after the coup, at the right time to turn the workers away from social revolution. That's why the workers turned their attention back 500 years, and the Hussite revolution was interpreted as a theological revolution [...] to build the machinery of their own enslavement."[5]

The Soviet Hussites overthrew the bourgeois tyranny of the Empire to create a classless, ultimately pan-European peace. "You, thousands and thousands of simple citizens," Gottwald proclaimed. "You have saved our country from the new Lipany [...] the decisive word is now in all questions of nation and state for the descendants of the real Táborites, followers of Master Jan Hus, Jan Zižka of Trochno, Prokop Holý, and Rohač of Duba."[6] One of the great cultural achievements of Soviet Hussitism is the film trilogy of Otakar Vávra, *Jan Hus*, *Jan Žižka*, and *Proti Vsem* (Against All) made between 1953 and 1957. These are easily available on YouTube, and even for viewers unable to understand the Czech, they embody Soviet historiographic appropriation of the national mythos. Red predominates among the Hussite soldiers, and how can a peasant army not march into battle without such instruments of labour as sickles or hammers. The enemy rides against the Hussites bedecked in black tabards with white crosses, or white tabards with black ones, because they are Germans. Never mind that these are the colours of the Teutonic knights,

---

**5** From Klement Gottlwalt, *Spisy* 14 (1958), quoted in Bohumir Janoušek, "Husitská Myšlenka v boji za mir a přatelstvi mezi narodý" *Husitsky Tábor* 4 (1981): 9-20 at 14.

**6** Quoted in Josef Macek, *Tábor v Husitském Revolučním Hnuti*, 2 vols. (Prague: Czech Academy of Sciences, 1952 and 1955), 1:29. Macek himself was the eminent Czech Soviet scholar of Hussitism, and his *The Hussite Movement in Bohemia*, 2nd ed. (Prague: Orbis, 1958), is one of the few English-language overviews of Hussitism.

and not the Holy Roman Empire. The same actor plays both Hus and Žižka, and while he does his best to evoke pious martyrdom in the former role, he clearly much prefers the latter, where he is given the freedom to make liberal use of his mace.

The two most important historians of Hussitism in the Soviet period, among many contenders, are Josef Macek and Robert Kalivoda. For both, the Hussite movement represents the crisis of feudalism that had been building for several centuries across Europe. This allowed the designation "revolution" to be applied to the Hussites, which in Marxism means that the Hussites represent a signal point in human history. Two classes were engaged in the Hussite movement, Macek argued, the Prague university masters, merchants, and lower nobility, and the Tábor peasant workers. In Marxist terms, this made for a combination of the bourgeoisie from Prague and the proletariat from Tábor. Inevitably, the two factions would have disparate goals. The Prague element was inevitably set on constructing an economic structure independent of hegemonic control from Empire and Church, while the Táborites intended an antifeudal, chiliastic social structure in which property ownership was recognized as foreign to the human condition. Macek's remarkable economic analysis of Tábor includes extensive records of the material history of the city, well past the defeat of Lipany and into the period in which the town was regarded as a self-governing entity. The little available in English written during the Soviet period gives no indication of the great effort scholars exerted in recovering the social, economic, and historical evidence for the Hussite movement. In fact, the state-sponsored historical museum, the *Muzea husitského revolučniho hnuti*, has been publishing the proceedings of regular conferences sponsored by the government since 1978, entitled *Husitský Tábor*. This series contains extensive research into the Hussite movement that is invaluable to the study of the period, and reflects the changing interests and ideological approaches that have defined Czech scholarship for the past four decades.

The Soviet-era scholarship is particularly hampered by an almost uniform colour blindness regarding theology. Robert

Kalivoda provides a good example. He argued that the idea of the bourgeoisie arose from the mass production of weaponry, material goods explicitly designed to maintain civil order and consent to ideological domination of the feudal system. But the need for mass-produced weapons to arm an increasingly large soldiery meant a non-agricultural production economy and an increase in mercantile exchange of goods. Before this, the idea of capital was not needed, Kalivoda reasoned, but with the rise of large armies in the later medieval period, the necessary supplies and specialized weapons, armour, and transportation required the more complex economic levels of exchange that introduce proto-capitalism. The Hussites, he argued, began to unfold the antifeudal social network that would eventually become the bourgeoisie through its anti-feudal ideology, and its generation of need for large armies to engage with them. The emergence of the bourgeoisie was not a single act that occurred at the birth of Modernity, but a process that began with the Hussite rejection of a feudal church and the inevitability of inheritance of a crown, and continued into the much larger effects of the Peasants' War of the Reformation.

Kalivoda perceived a tension underlying Hussite theology, between two opposing forces. On the one side, Hus and the more conventional theologians, who represent rationalism and humanism and, on the other, Tábor and, more to the point, the Pickhart position as described by its opponents, which he calls pantheist. For Kalivoda, the Pickhart zeal for eliminating all private property, civil gender norms, sexual restrictions, and "naturalism" represents the logical final development of the Táborite idealism. This tendency, he argues, is based in the philosophical realism that is the foundation for all Hussite theology. Wyclif and Hus perceived an ideal reality, yet remained monotheists unwilling to trace out the ultimately pantheistic conclusions of their realism, fearful of the elimination of the divine transcendence. "In the last phase of rural proletarian Hussitism is manifest the natural God–man, whom we have already met in the teachings of the Free Spirit sect, yet not as the ideal of a fully developed robust individual man, but as a social category that frees all from human suffering."[7] It is particularly easy to see how Tábor appeared favourable in a Marxist reading of history in interpretations that discard theology as not really what everybody was thinking about, and not worth understanding by a respectable historian.

The end of Soviet domination meant a change to the understanding of the Hussites in Czechoslovakia, and after 1994, the Czech Republic. The dominant scholar has been František Šmahel, whose 1993 *Husitská revoluce*, published in German in 2002 as *Die Hussitische Revolution*, covers the socio-economic background, the history of the movement itself, and the historiographical role it has played in Czech cultural identity. His many articles and other monographs have played an important role in shifting the direction of Czech scholarship to align with contemporary Western academic standards, and his many students continue to develop the study of the Hussites and incorporate it into the ongoing scholarly dialogue about the later medieval period. The reader is advised to investigate the proceedings of the biennial conferences sponsored by the Czech Academy and organized under the title "Bohemian Reformation and Religious Practice." The moving force behind these conferences has been David Holeton, whose work in Hussite worship, liturgy, and hymnody has been very important for the understanding of the movement as it was experienced by its adherents and its opponents. At its website, www.brrp.org, the most recent ideas and research on the Hussites is available, translated into English by Dr. Zdenek David. Additionally, the Centre for Medieval Studies at Charles University has a very wide range of otherwise difficult to find resources, from Palacký's *Fontes rerum bohemicarum* to the many ground-breaking editions of Hussite theologians, which continues to grow. This can be found online as Czech medieval sources online under the Centrum medievistých studii [http://147.231.53.91/src/index.php?s=v&cat=11].

---

**7** Robert Kalivoda, *Das Hussitische Denken im Lichte seiner Quellen* (Berlin: Akademie, 1969), 80–81.

The partisan nature of Hussite scholarship over the past two centuries is difficult to avoid. In a very real sense, its evolution follows the changing nature of the Czech lands, from nascent Czech nationalism in a time of Austro-Hungarian hegemony, to the establishment of a post-1918 Czechoslovakian identity, to the pan-Slavic Communist ideology that the Soviets used to give historical foundation to their domination of central Europe. Just as Prague and Tábor fought bitterly for ownership of the ideals represented by Hus at Konstanz, so the political forces of the twentieth century struggled for claim to the final word on the Hussites. The present state of the Czechs is that of a small, independent country in Central Europe, divided between Prague, with its eyes on the global West, and much of the rest of the country, with its remnant nostalgia for the stability of Soviet rule. The scholars now active in studying the Hussites continue to work to separate themselves from the duelling ideologies of the past century, while retaining respect for figures like Šmahel, who was compelled to continue his scholarship while being a tram conductor during an especially difficult point in the Soviet control of Prague.

Conclusion

# Classifying the Hussites: Revolutions and Fundamentalism

The possibilities for scholarly work on the Hussites are manifold, and thanks to the wealth of primary texts now readily available, are ripe for development. Additionally, the growing list of manuscripts on such electronic portals as the Enrich Manuscriptorium [manuscriptorium.com] invites the creation of editions of the great number of unedited primary sources, both in Latin and in Old Czech. As the historiography of the Hussites suggests, classifying the movement involves exploring one's own intellectual assumptions about social structure, social movements, and religious identity. Two questions arise: do the Hussites represent a revolution, and were they fundamentalist? Both seem particularly appropriate for our society, which continues to experience repercussions from the events in the Muslim world that are frequently described using both of these terms.

Jacques Derrida argued in his 1994 *Spectres of Marx* that the fall of the Soviet Union and Marxism as defined during the twentieth-century Cold War did not make Marx irrelevant or wrong. In fact, Marxism is now open to a reinterpretation given the confusing new realities introduced by globalism. Students of Derrida now perceive a new reaction to the crises and ambiguities consequent to the rise of corporations that are more powerful than nations. The species of revolution populating post-1989 history include populist rejections of state corruption, "fundamentalist" religious reaction to secularism, post-colonial recovery of popular identities—all of them valid means by which to describe Hussitism. The Marxist reading of revolt as a bottom-up reformulation of social structure has realized new dimensions with the end of the nation state as the main unit of social organization.[1] The Hussites provide a good example by which to explore these new dimensions.

But many other social revolts had occurred in Europe before 1419, and the legitimacy of using the term "revolution" to describe the Hussites in a post-Soviet worldview is open to doubt. The thirteenth and fourteenth centuries saw popular revolts in English, Italian, French, and Flemish lands, revolts against king, emperor, and pope, and against the colonial control of one city or feudal holding over another. The radical Franciscans, the Cathars, and other lesser known religious minorities generated church-sponsored crusades within Europe long before trouble started in Bohemia.[2] What separates the many instances of revolt from the Hussite movement is the latter's adoption of a developed ideology. Howard Kaminsky argued that this ideology is directly tied to the first true European ideology of revolution, that of John Wyclif. Wyclif's understanding of the right working of society involved complete restructuring of both secular and sacred realms of power, a rejection of the feudal system, and the creation of a Christian kingdom unlike anything that had existed, "translating," in Kaminsky's words, "reformation into revolution."[3] When Wycliffism made

---

1 See Richard Gillman-Opalsky, *Spectres of Revolt* (London: Repeater, 2016).

2 Samuel K. Cohn Jr., *Lust for Liberty: The Politics of Social Revolt in Medieval Europe 1200–1425* (Cambridge, MA: Harvard University Press, 2006) covers these, but oddly pays no attention to the Hussites.

3 Howard Kaminsky, "Wycliffism as Ideology of Revolution," *Church History* 32, no. 1 (March 1963): 57–74 at 70. See also the beginning of his 1967 *The Hussite Revolution*. His most carefully considered assessment of the place of the Hussites in history can be found in his "The Problematics of 'Heresy' and 'The Reformation'," in *Häresie und vorzeitige Reformation im Spätmittelalter*, ed. František Šmahel and Elisabeth Müller-Luckner (München: Oldenbourg,

its impact into Bohemian society, it resonated in university halls, pulpits, and palaces, across social classes, catalyzing extant reform elements into a revolutionary movement.

Kaminsky's position was certainly a product of his years in Prague immediately following the Second World War. At that point, the term "revolution" became the standard designator for the Hussite phenomenon, as described above. To a Marxist reader of history like Josef Macek, Hussitism, specifically Tábor, represented the first true evidence of class struggle defining the ultimate destruction of hegemonic oppression. Hannah Arendt, on the other hand, dismissed the idea of a Christian revolution in 1962. "The fact is that no revolution was ever made in the name of Christianity prior to the modern age."[4] The Augustinian "Two Cities" model of history meant that the *novus ordo seculorum* that the revolution ushers in can only be the establishment of Christ's kingdom on earth, the end of the City of Man, which eliminates the prospects of a historically identifiable revolution. It is only with secularization, she argues, the separation of religion from politics, that something new can be birthed into human history. Kaminsky once reflected in private conversation that his 1963 article was a response to Arendt's argument.

Another question that has arisen in the past two decades is whether or not the Hussites in general, and Tábor in particular, would qualify as the Christian fundamentalist prototype for the Taliban or Al-Qaeda. Many scholars and others familiar with the history of Tábor in particular have voiced this opinion in informal conversation. The informed understanding of fundamentalism as a twentieth-century phenomenon naturally would discount this as historically anachronistic, selecting several familiar characteristics shared by contemporary movements and the Hussites without remembering that five

---

1998), where he argues that the terms "heresy" and "reformation" impede a fuller understanding of European Christianity in general, and the Hussites in particular.

**4** Hannah Arendt, *On Revolution* (Harmondsworth: Penguin, 1977), 17.

centuries separate them. It might be acceptable to give Tábor honorary membership in the genus of fundamentalism by referring to it as a proto-fundamentalist movement, but to do more would be to demand that the concept of fundamentalism be completely overhauled. But it has recently been suggested that using the term "fundamentalism" as an umbrella term, or a general term including distinct species variations in different religious traditions, is deeply problematic in itself. The Hussite phenomenon lends itself to this discussion.

The Fundamentalism Project sponsored by the American Academy of Arts and Sciences produced five volumes, edited by Martin Marty and R. Scott Appleford, that have given rise to considerable discussion about how to study a religious group's reaction to a society it perceives to be at odds with its core principles. This is certainly a common occurrence in history, so Marty and Appleford stipulate nine characteristics that identify a movement to be fundamentalist. These include (i) reactivity to the secular marginalization of religion; (ii) selectivity in defining religious doctrine; (iii) moral manichaeism (that is, a stark delineation of an us versus them ethical systems); (iv) doctrinal inerrancy and absolutism; (v) millennialism and messianism; (vi) elect membership defining the favoured group, (vii) stark boundaries between the personal identities of members and non-members; (viii) rigid authoritarian organization; and (ix) strict behavioural requirements. As the preceding narrative suggests, Tábor fits each of these admirably, with the exception of the first criterion. Secularism was then not a factor in European civilization; as Charles Taylor describes it, fifteenth-century Europe remained in the pre-modern state, defined by a dominant belief in spiritual forces acting in the world, in which two temporal structures, the sacred and the profane, are active, and a cosmic teleology defining all human action.[5] If the Modern,

---

**5** Charles Taylor, *A Secular Age* (Cambridge, MA: Harvard University Press, 2007), 61, from his summary of chap. 1. Taylor's description of the secular worldview is as controversial as the Fundamentalism Project has been; for medievalists, in its overly simplified descri-

by which post-Enlightenment secularism is understood, is the necessary condition for the genesis of fundamentalism, one can hardly argue that Tábor is fundamentalist.

David Harrington Watts has recently argued that the term "fundamentalism" is a secular pejorative term intended to reduce religious movements that challenge "our" values, the post-Enlightenment self-evident truths defining the Liberal Society. In so doing, the term forces a host of religious movements from cultures around the world onto the Procrustean bed constructed by twentieth-century non-denominational evangelical Protestants when they invented the term "Fundamentalism," despite the many cultural differences that may separate them. It is a kind of colonialism convinced that any ideology that questions the base values of the West must be extirpated, as has been demonstrated in the United States with its "war on terrorism" directed expressly towards Muslim militant movements. Included in Watts's critique of the concept of "fundamentalism" is a frustration with how the term "modern" is defined. There is, after all, quite a long period of time between the development of the intellectual tradition that led to the seventeenth-century Enlightenment in Europe, and the establishment of a secular Europe. Were the Thirty Years' War "modern" simply because Descartes was writing during that horror?

The use of the term "modern" was, as medievalists well know, common from the twelfth century onwards. It was first used to describe the *logica modernorum* in which supposition theory developed and led to the sophisticated advances in Aristotelian logic and semantics of the thirteenth and fourteenth centuries. At the beginning of the fourteenth century, the term "modern" was being used to refer to the Ockhamist philosophical movement, in which the logic employed by natural philosophers was argued to be entirely different from the logic of revealed Christian theology. Readers familiar with Heiko Obermann's *Harvest of Medieval Theology* will recall the

ption of what appears to be an arbitrary choice for the beginning of Modernity.

zeal with which Obermann argued for the importance of this species of thought in understanding Protestantism. Foremost among the critics of the "modern" was John Wyclif, who sneeringly referred to them as "doctors of signs" throughout his philosophical works. Wyclif venerated the theological worldview of the twelfth-century Neoplatonists of Paris, in which the whole of reality is contained within the Word of God and is revealed by Grace favoured through divine illumination. And Wyclif's view, as described above, was critically important for the articulation of the theology that would be associated with the Hussites in general, and with Tábor in particular.

Tábor's open disdain for the "modern" crops up most often in the writings of its chief theologian, Nicholas Biskupec. He provides an especially useful example in his *Confessio Táboritarum*, where he contrasts the *fundamentum* of the Prague Masters, Rokycana in particular, with the *fundamentum* of Tábor.[6] Rokycana's *fundamentum* is the position that the church ought not be ruled only by the authority of Scripture, but also by the four Latin Fathers (Augustine, Jerome, Ambrose, and Gregory), as well as pontifexes "predisposed to the exposition of Holy Scripture," synods, and councils ruling in agreement with the Latin Fathers. The Fathers, Biskupec continues, are to be preferred "as opposed to the thousand other Modern expositors and interpreters infected with the ambition of the age." Tábor, on the other hand, "prefers to proceed in a way most certain and secure, in which path we may not be led astray eternally [...] the final resolution of all difficulties about truth that may arise we posit to be the law of God, the works of Christ, and of the primitive and apostolic church." The Church Fathers used the same foundation for their reasoning, he explains, so there is no need to regard their writings as having equal authority to Scripture. Biskupec cites Wyclif's *De veritate Sacrae Scripturae*

---

**6** Biskupec's Latin term *fundamentum* means foundation, groundwork, or base, and his use employs a building metaphor, describing the foundation upon which each side builds the edifice of its theology.

throughout his description of Tábor's *fundamentum*, specifically his argument for the primacy of Scripture in governing the faith in *De veritate Sacrae Scripturae* I, chap. 10. Here, Wyclif himself uses the term *fundamentum* in explaining why we should believe in the hypostatic union of Christ, "the faith in scripture is the foundation by which the same should be known."[7] I believe the argument can be made that the definition that restricts "fundamentalism" to the twentieth century is shown to be misguided given Biskupec's use of the term *fundamentum* in his description of the differences between Tábor, Prague, and the Roman church, and his specific aim at the *moderni*, who are guilty of pursuing their own interpretations based in their secular pursuits. This is not the place for making that argument, though; it is enough to show here that the phenomenon of Tábor provides us with a rich ground for understanding the limits of terms like "revolution" and "fundamentalism," now commonly used to distinguish the Modern from the Pre-Modern.

My hope, as I mentioned at the outset, is that this very brief sketch elicits interest to engage in a deeper study of the Hussite phenomenon. The Czech scholarship on the subject is fascinating, and given the relatively small number of its practitioners and readers, filled with the kind of side-comments and fiery arguments that evoke their subjects' own discourse. One cannot truly engage in studying the Hussites without some ability to read Czech, but this is now much easier than it once was. The Hussite primary sources are in both Latin and Old Czech. The Latin is standard fifteenth-century scholarly and diplomatic language, but the Old Czech can be lively and earthy, very much worth the trouble it takes to learn it. While many of the primary sources have been edited, many more remain unedited, in need of scholars willing to transcribe, collate, and interpret the texts. The Czech scholarship deserves a much wider audience, and many of the landmark texts deserve translation into more widely read languages.

---

**7** See *Confessio Taboritarum*, ed. Amedeo Molnar and Romolo Cegna (Rome: Istituto storico italiano per il Medio Evo, 1983), 144–52.

Additionally, the Latin primary sources would find many more readers in translation. As fifteenth-century studies advance, and as more scholars turn to Central and Eastern Europe, the Hussites will continue to be regarded as of great importance and truly interesting, not for their effect on Modernity, but in their own right.

# Further Reading

## Primary Sources

For edited sources, the reader is referred to the web portal http://147.231.53.91/src/index.php?s=v&cat=49, hosted by the Centrum Medievistických Studii in Prague. The complete works of Hus, Matěj of Janov, Chelčický, and many of the works of Jakoubek, Rokycana, Biskupec, and others described in these pages are available here.

## Studies in English

Bartoš, F. M. *The Hussite Revolution 1424–1437*. Translated by R. Klassen. Boulder: East European Monographs, 1986.

> The second half of Bartoš's celebrated history of the Hussites, *Husitská revoluce*, translated into English.

Fudge, Thomas. *Jan Hus: Religious Reform and Social Revolution in Bohemia*. London, I. B. Tauris, 2010.

> Complete, albeit occasionally controversial, biography of Hus.

——. *Jerome of Prague and the Foundations of the Hussite Movement*. Oxford: Oxford University Press, 2016.

> First English language monograph of this important figure.

——. *The Trial of Jan Hus: Medieval Heresy and Criminal Procedure*. Oxford: Oxford University Press, 2013.

> Argues for the legitimacy of Hus's conviction for heresy.

Heymann, Frederick G. *George of Bohemia, King of Heretics*. Princeton: Princeton University Press, 1965.

Overview of the life and reign of Jiří Poděbradý.

———. *John Žižka and the Hussite Revolution*. Princeton: Princeton University Press, 1955.

Definitive biography of the general, eminently readable.

Kaminsky, Howard. *A History of the Hussite Revolution*. Berkeley: University of California Press, 1967.

This remains the essential English language account of the movement to 1425.

Kejř, Jiří. *The Hussites*. Prague: Panorama, 1984.

Excellent overview of the movement, translated from the Czech *Husité*, but less theology and hard to find.

Macek, Josef. *The Hussite Movement in Bohemia*, Prague: Orbis, 1953.

English language version of the official Soviet version of the Hussites. The generous use of red ink is not accidental.

Soukup, Pavel, and Michael van Dussen, eds. *Companion to the Hussites*. Brill's Companions to the Christian Tradition. Leiden: Brill, forthcoming.

Contains essays on the Hussites from many active scholars.

Šmahel, František, and Ota Pavlíček, eds. *Companion to Jan Hus*. Brill's Companions to the Christian Tradition. Leiden: Brill, 2015.

Contains recent essays on many aspects of Hus life, thought, influence.

Wagner, Murray L. *Petr Chelčický. A Radical Separatist in Hussite Bohemia*. Studies in Mennonite and Anabaptist History. Scottdale: Herald, 1983.

Only English language overview of Chelčický, good summaries of his works.

# Non-English Works

Bartoš, F. M. *Čechy v době Husově, 1378–1415*. Prague: Laichter, 1947.

Intellectual, historical background for the Hussite phenomenon.

——. *Husitská revoluce, I: Doba Žižkova 1415–1426 / F.M. Bartoš*. Prague: Czech Academy of Sciences, 1965

The Hussite war to 1425.

Boubín, Jaroslav. *Petr Chelčický: Myslitel a reformátor*. Prague: Vyšehrad, 2012

Introduction to Chelčický by his modern editor.

Cermanová, Pavlína. *Čechy na konci věků: apokalyptické myšlení a vize husitské doby*. Prague: Argo, 2013

Recent overview of millennialism at the heart of Hussite theology.

De Vooght, Paul. *Jacobellus de Stříbro, 142 : premier théologien du hussitisme* . Leuven: Revue d'histoire ecclésiastique, 1972.

Excellent introduction to Jakoubek.

Herold, Vilém. *Pražská Univerzita a Wyclif: Wyclifovo učení o ideách a geneze husitského revolučního myšlení*. Prague: Univerzita Karlova, 1985

Collection of essays on Wycliffism in Prague up to its condemnation in 1410.

Höfler, Karl Adolf Constantin von. *Geschichtsschreiber der hussitischen Bewegung in Böhmen*. 3 vols. Vienna: Hof- und Staatsdruckerei, 1856–1866.

Useful collection of documents compiled by a notorious critic, including Laurence of Březova's *Chronicle* and Biskupec's *Chronicon Táboritorum*.

Macek, Josef. *Tábor v Husitském Revolučním Hnuti*. 2 vols. Prague: Czech Academy of Sciences, 1952 and 1955.

The Soviet history of Tábor, filled with economic and social details.

Šmahel, František. *Husitská revoluce*. 4 vols. Prague: Historický, 1993. Translated by Thomas Krzenck as *Die Hussitische Revolution*. 3 vols. Hannover: Hahn 2002.

The definitive history of the Hussites

Soukup, Pavel. *Reformní kazatelství a Jakoubek ze Stříbra*. Prague: Filosofia, 2011.

Recent study of Jakoubek as preacher showing recognition of the importance of theology to Hussitism.

Printed and bound by CPI Group (UK) Ltd, Croydon, CR0 4YY

12/06/2024

14514473-0003